TIMBER PRESS
POCKET GUIDE TO
Bulbs

TIMBER PRESS
POCKET GUIDE TO

Bulbs

JOHN E. BRYAN, F.I. HORT.

TIMBER PRESS

Photos by author unless otherwise indicated.

Frontispiece: *Leucojum aestivum,* also known as summer snowflake (Jack Hobbs)

Published in 2005 by

Timber Press, Inc.
The Haseltine Building
133 S.W. Second Avenue, Suite 450
Portland, Oregon 97204-3527, U.S.A.

www.timberpress.com

Printed through Colorcraft Ltd., Hong Kong

Library of Congress Cataloging-in-Publication Data

Bryan, John E., 1931-
    Timber Press pocket guide to bulbs / John E. Bryan, F.I. Hort.
        p. cm. — (Timber Press pocket guides)
    Includes bibliographical references (p.   ) and index.
    ISBN 0-88192-725-2 (flexibind)
    1. Bulbs. I. Hort, F. I. II. Title. III. Series.
    SB425.B753 2005
    635.9'4--dc22
                                                    2004028006

A catalog record for this book is also available from the British Library.

Acknowledgments

Thanks again to all those people and places mentioned in *Bulbs* (2002), on which this pocket guide is based. Special thanks to the individuals and organizations who provided photographs for this guide, specifically the Alpine Garden Society (United Kingdom), Maurice Boussard, Sally Ferguson, Harry B. Hay, Jack Hobbs, Klehm's Song Sparrow Perennial Farm, Chris Lovell, Eddie McRae, the International Flower Bulb Center (Netherlands), the late Robert Ornduff, the Helen Crocker Russell Library, W. George Schmid, Katarina Stenman, Arne Strid, and David M. Ward. I also thank my editor, Linda J. Willms, and all the Timber Press staff who made this book possible.

About This Book

The entries in this pocket guide are arranged in alphabetical order by scientific name. The alphabetical list includes information on well-known plant genera with bulbs, corms, tubers, or rhizomes except for orchids, gingers, waterlilies and other aquatic plants, peonies, and hostas. If a genus or species name appears to be missing from this alphabetical listing, it may be because the name has been changed by taxonomists. To find the current name, look up the "missing" name in the Index. Cultivar names are enclosed by single quotation marks. Zone numbers refer to the lowest USDA cold-hardiness zone in which the bulbs will survive.

CONTENTS

Opposite: *Lilium* 'Compass', Asiatic hybrid (Jack Hobbs)

PREFACE

I cannot claim that my fascination with bulbs, in the broadest definition of the word, came at the start of my career in horticulture in 1946. As an apprentice in a nursery located in Devon, England, I was introduced to the wonderful world of plants by having to water tomatoes in greenhouses for six solid weeks. For this work 48 hours each week, I received the princely sum of 10 shillings, roughly $1.25 per week.

Having survived this period and having learned a great deal about the culture of tomatoes, I was assigned the job of preparing bulbs for forcing. There were no special chambers with controlled temperatures and humidity at that time. Rather, we used the old method, still in use today, of plunging the bulbs into beds and covering them with sand and soil. The interest in the miracles that can be forced upon a bulb, in this case tulips, hyacinths, daffodils, and crocuses, has remained with me to this day.

While a student at the Royal Botanic Garden, Edinburgh, Scotland, and during postgraduate studies that followed at the Royal Horticultural Society's Garden at Wisley, Surrey, England; at The Hague in the Netherlands; and in Paris, France, bulbs were never far from my mind. My interest was heightened when I first saw the magnificent colors of the bulb fields in the Netherlands. This was reinforced when I came to the United States in 1961 to work at Jan de Graaff's Oregon Bulb Farms near Portland. Here, the raising of many new lily hybrids and their introduction into commerce fascinated me.

Over the years it has been my good fortune to have known and worked with such great men in the lily world as Jan de Graaff, Earl Hornback, Harold Comber, and Edward McRae, with whom I was a student at the Royal Botanic Garden, Edinburgh, and who is the originator of many fine new hybrid lilies. My association with these fine horticulturists and my past experience stood me in good stead when, while I was the director of the Strybing Arboretum and Botanic Gardens in Golden Gate Park in San Francisco, California, we undertook experimental plantings of many different bulbs, recording their growth patterns, time of flowering, height at flowering, and so on.

Since that time I have visited many other parts of the world and have seen bulbs growing in the wild. To my mind this is the best way to understand the cultural needs of any plant and also to gain a greater perspective of the enormous numbers of species.

This pocket guide, like the encyclopedia on which it is based, is intended to give gardeners a greater appreciation of bulbs. It is hoped that the information contained herein will be both useful and enjoyable to the reader. Nothing I write here, however, can accomplish this as well as the thrill of watching bulbs grow and each year witnessing their dazzling displays of brilliance, often with little effort on the part of the gardener.

If I have encouraged but one person to grow these wondrous plants who has never done so, then I will have achieved my purpose and the effort will have been more than worthwhile.

Opposite: *Iris pseudacorus* 'Variegata' (Jack Hobbs)

INTRODUCTION

Mention the word *bulb* to people and a range of plants comes to mind, including crocuses, dahlias, gladiolus, irises, lilies, tulips, and many others. Some are true bulbs; others are corms, rhizomes, and tubers but fall under the umbrella term *bulbous plants*.

A **true bulb** consists of a stem and leaves adapted for storage. The stem is compressed into a flattened plate, and the modified, fleshy leaves are filled with food reserves. Tulips, hyacinths, and daffodils have **tunicated bulbs** in which the leaves are layered closely around each other, the outermost leaves forming a tunic around the bulb, with the outer leaves often dry and brown. Lilies and fritillaries have **scaly bulbs** in which the leaves overlap each other but do not form a tunic, and are more succulent.

A **corm** is a stem, swollen and modified for storage. The usually rounded stem is flattened on top and slightly concave beneath. Frequently it has a brown skin, not dissimilar to the tunic of a true bulb. Upon being cut, however, the corm will appear solid. On the basal plate, young, small corms known as cormels will arise. Two examples of corms are the crocus and the gladiolus.

A **rhizome** is a swollen underground stem (sometimes breaking the surface of the soil) from the ends of which shoots emerge. Roots are produced on the underside; side branches will be formed which have leaves with roots on the undersides and foliage at their ends. The most commonly recognized rhizome is the iris, although some iris species are true bulbs.

A **tuber** also is a swollen underground stem, but not the base of a stem. It is usually fleshy, rounded, and covered with scaly leaves, often minute and concentrated toward the top of the tuber. In the axils, eyes develop which produce the stems. Two examples are the tuberous begonia and dahlia.

Dormancy

Despite their great diversity of color, flower form, size, habitat, and growing conditions, most bulbous plants have a dormant period brought about by prevailing growing conditions, such as the heat and dryness of summer or the extreme cold (accompanied by snow) of winter. A bulb becomes dormant when climatic conditions impose that state and such ceasing of active growth will not cause it harm. Dormancy can be imposed by withholding moisture, for example, but at a given point dictated by its internal clock, a bulb will become dormant with or without water.

Certain interior activities continue during dormancy, as they are a necessary part of the life cycle. Evergreen bulbs (those that become dormant without shedding their foliage) reach their dormant period when climatic conditions **and** the interior cyclical clock dictate it. Dormancy then is that part of the life cycle belonging to a definite chronological cycle, in all bulbs, evergreen or not.

Daffodils and squills make a great early season color combination. (International Flower Bulb Center)

Opposite: *Kniphofia uvaria*

11

Cultivation

Bulbs should be planted in soil cultivated about 12 inches (30 cm) deep. Adding organic matter improves soil: it binds sandy soil, thus increasing moisture retention, and it loosens clay, allowing air to enter and water to drain. Well-rotted compost and manure are both excellent organic additives. Avoid unrotted compost and fresh manure. Apply a general fertilizer (10–10–10) and rake it into the surface. Allow the soil to settle for a day or two so air pockets are eliminated.

Many bulbs require deep planting. Indeed, the most common mistake made is planting at an incorrect depth. A rule of thumb is to place the bulb at a depth of three times its height; for example, a 1-inch (2.5-cm) bulb should be planted with 3 inches (7.5 cm) of soil over it.

Planting

There are many ways to plant bulbs. Bulb planters, which remove a core of soil, often have a marker on the side that enables a hole of correct depth to be made. A trowel can also be used.

For small bulbs or large plantings, remove all the soil (to the planting depth) from the area to space the bulbs evenly. Nestle the bulbs firmly but without excessive pressure. Finally, cover them with soil, but do not compact it. If annuals are to be planted over the bulbs, use a planting board to prevent undue soil compaction.

Water in newly planted bulbs to eliminate air pockets. Apply a mulch to preserve moisture and reduce weeds. The taller the flower spikes, the deeper the mulch—2 or 3 inches (5–7.5 cm) for taller bulbs, about 1 inch (2.5 cm) for shorter

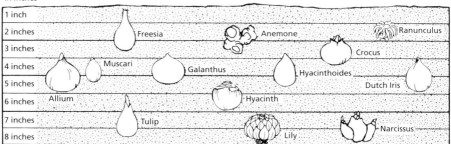

Planting depths for selected spring-flowering bulbs. These should be planted in September or October where there is frost, in warmer climes in November or December. Flowering times vary according to variety.

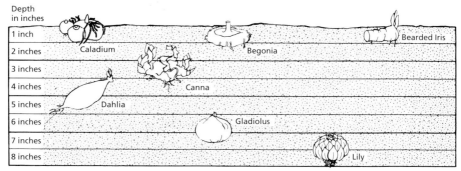

Planting depths for selected summer-flowering bulbs. These should be planted about two weeks before the last frost.

ones. Crocuses and other small bulbs should be covered with a finer grade of mulch than daffodils or tulips. Mulch minimizes constant thawing and freezing of the soil, which causes heaving, which in turn breaks the roots and forms air pockets under the bulbs. Shallowly planted bulbs are especially susceptible.

Planted bulbs require little attention until new seasonal growth appears above the soil. At that time, apply a general fertilizer (10–10–10). In rainy climates, the fertilizer will be washed into the soil; in dry climates, water it in. Give a second feeding three or four weeks after the first one. For spring-flowering bulbs, two feedings are sufficient.

Lifting and Storing

Daffodils, hyacinths, and tulips planted in the border should be lifted when the foliage becomes unsightly. Remove the bulbs from the ground with foliage still attached and allow them to dry in a cool, airy place. When the foliage has died down, remove it and any remaining soil. Examine the bulbs, discarding those unsound or bruised. Store bulbs at 60°F (16°C) where air can circulate freely. During the summer, check periodically for rotting or spoiled bulbs.

Precooling

In colder climates where soil temperatures are low, no precooling is necessary. In warmer climates, bulbs planted in fall should first be precooled. This applies especially to tulips. Start precooling six to eight weeks before the soil temperatures are the same as, or a little lower than, the precooling temperature of around 45°F (7°C).

Summer-flowering Bulbs

Plant summer-flowering and frost-tender bulbs two weeks before the last frost is expected. If the ground is cold the bulbs will not grow, so delay planting if there is any chance of a late frost. In warm regions, plant in March or April. Summer-flowering bulbs need good day length to grow well. Start begonias, caladiums, and dahlias in a greenhouse, frame, or well-lighted garage to

Begonias are popular summer-flowering plants in warmer climates.

speed the first flowering. Never expose started bulbs to frost.

Bulbs in continuous growth, such as begonias and dahlias, benefit from feedings of liquid fertilizer each month, stopping six weeks before the bulbs are to be lifted. In warmer regions, where dahlias are left in the ground overwinter, a feeding of 0–10–10 in early September will increase the hardiness of the bulbs and reduce the possibility of rotting.

Bulbs to be lifted and stored overwinter should be allowed to ripen by withholding water toward the end of summer. The first frost often is a light one, enough to burn the foliage but not harm the bulbs themselves. The bulbs then should be protected or moved to a frost-free location.

Store gladiolus in paper sacks with holes or in nets to ensure air circulation. Store begonias, caladiums, cannas, and dahlias in barely moist peat, so the roots will not lose moisture and be plump when planting time comes around. The ideal temperature for storing summer-flowering bulbs is 40° to 45°F (4°–7°C). Protect stored bulbs from rodents. Label the bulbs as to color prior to lifting to ensure good planting arrangements in the spring.

Bulbs in the Landscape

Among the many plants in gardens and woodland areas, few add focal points as effectively as bulbous plants when correctly selected. Crocuses in a lawn can add interest in early spring. Daffodils near a rose bed give color before they face the competition of the roses. Bluebells are superb in a woodland, where their messy foliage is not a problem as it is in formal borders. Summer-flowering lilies prolong the season of interest and color in a shrub border, and containers of flowering bulbs add color to decks and terraces.

Naturalizing Bulbs in Grass

The more effective bulbs for naturalizing are *Narcissus* among taller-growing grasses and *Crocus* in a lawn or shorter grasses. Select a location carefully. Crocuses require viewing from a close range, small-flowered daffodils from a little farther away, and the large-flowered cultivars from even a greater distance. Bluebells (*Hyacinthoides* spp.) look best in drifts under small trees or among or in front of large shrubs.

A scene of naturalized bulbs is more effective on a slope or undulating ground than on level ground. Even a slight rise will afford better drainage and present a better staging; the eye is then able to appreciate the entire planting. The same applies to undulating ground, where the plantings should be on the slopes and crests, not in the valleys. The direction in which the slope faces is of lesser importance; it should not be exposed to much wind, which can flatten the flowers, especially when accompanied by rain.

Set the bulbs in a random pattern. The outline should be free-form—the shape of a cloud, not a square or circle. Naturalized plantings can be made of a mixture of early, mid season, and late-flowering bulbs.

A drift of English bluebells, *Hyacinthoides non-scripta*

Attention to the culture of the bulbs each year, while minimal, should not be neglected. Allow for a last cutting of the grass just as the first bulbs appear through the soil. As soon as several bulbs have appeared, give them a dressing of 12–12–12 or a similarly balanced fertilizer. The spring rains should wash the fertilizer into the soil; if no rain is expected, water it into the soil. In heavy soils such feeding is not as essential as on sandy soils.

To maintain the vigor of bulbs naturalized in grass, allow the foliage to mature. Unfortunately this means the plantings can become unsightly by the end of spring and early summer, another reason for careful site selection.

Bulbs in the Woodland

Cardiocrinums, daffodils, fritillaries, lilies, and trilliums are superb in woodland areas. English bluebells are at home in such surroundings but must be planted in large quantities to be effective. *Cyclamen neapolitanum* does well at the base of a large tree but not too close to a tree or to a path.

Woodland plants, which can spread with surprising rapidity, should be seen and admired but not walked upon.

Select plants carefully. The upright-facing Asiatic lilies are too stiff and formal in a woodland, while the downward-facing *Lilium canadense* and *L. martagon* look at home in the woodland. The ideal location is an area where the lower part of the stem is shielded from the sun while the flowerhead is in some sun and seen against a background of foliage. Make sure lilies have room to spread, and plant a sufficient number so they will be a feature.

Cardiocrinum giganteum needs good moisture during the summer and, because it can reach well over 6 feet (1.8 m) tall, is ideal for an open glade. Autumn- and spring-flowering crocuses as well as colchicums need sunlight to perform well. Consider using them around the perimeter of woodland gardens.

Woodland bulbs have, for the most part, pendent flowers. Grape hyacinths (*Muscari* species) are an exception. They can be planted on the

Grape hyacinths (*Muscari* sp.) and double tulips (*Tulipa*, Parrot Group) at the famous Keukenhof Gardens in the Netherlands

edge of woodland areas, where they receive good sun. They are not effective unless planted in masses, but they grow well and multiply easily.

Bulbs in the Garden

No garden is too small to have at least a few bulbs. The smaller the area, the smaller the size of the plant; scale always is of importance.

While bulbs are frequently recommended for the perennial border, not all are suitable. The struggle for space and root competition may be too much, with the possible exception of dahlias, gladiolus, rhizomatous irises, and certain lilies. If no other space is available, then other bulbs can be grown in the perennial garden, but most deserve a place where they can be appreciated for their individual beauty. They should also be staged against complementary foliage, preferably not competing with perennials of equal height and strong color.

Anemones, bulbous irises, daffodils, freesias, gladiolus, large-flowered ornamental onions, ranunculus, and tulips lend a look of permanence in an annual border. Pink tulips above a bed of blue forget-me-nots, daffodils with pansies, large-flowered onions towering above taller-growing annuals, irises, and gladiolus—used not only for their color but also for their stiffer foliage—form grand contrasts.

The hyacinth, the most fragrant spring-flowering bulb, can be placed in groups near a window or close to an entrance, or in containers on the deck or patio. Color and fragrance are as much a part of the charm of bulbs as any other plants.

Bulbs for Cut Flowers

Bulbs grown for cut flowers are best in a location where, if they are cut, obvious gaps are avoided. Planting them very close together so the bulbs almost touch will allow for a selective cutting, with enough flowers left to remain attractive.

Amaryllis, anemones, daffodils, dahlias, freesias, gladiolus, irises, ixias, lilies, nerines, ranunculus, and tulips are all excellent cut flowers. Ornithogalums, while not commonly grown, will provide long-lasting flowers. Watsonias deserve to be more widely grown by home gardeners. Calla lilies are mainly associated with weddings

Irises growing in water at the Royal Botanic Garden, Edinburgh

A floral arrangement featuring Asiatic lilies

and funerals, but actually present a lovely display in the home, mixed with other flowers, and they last a long time.

When cutting flowers for the home, do not remove any more foliage than is absolutely necessary. The leaves manufacture the plant's food.

Container-Grown Bulbs

Certain bulbs, such as *Crocus*, *Hyacinthus*, and *Narcissus*, can be grown indoors without soil. Special vases are available, or you can fill a dish with pebbles, then add bulbs and more pebbles to keep the bulbs upright. After planting the bulbs, add water so that it almost, but not quite, touches the base of the bulbs. Place the vase or dish in the dark with temperatures between 45°F and 50°F (7°–10°C) until the bulbs have roots. When the roots emerge and top growth is made, give the bulbs room temperature and light.

Containers can be used effectively to grow bulbs, but they must be capable of holding enough soil to maintain fairly constant soil temperatures. If containers are too small and then are warmed by the sun, the soil temperature will reach

Freesias make excellent cut flowers. (Jack Hobbs)

Tulips are one of many bulbs suitable for a container.

a point which could harm the bulbs. If there is no room for a large container, then keep the smaller ones shaded to avoid extremes of temperature.

Drainage is essential; use a porous soil mix with a good organic content. The container should be deep enough to give the bulbs the desired depth of soil cover, as in the open ground. Having only a very small amount of room—be it verandah, deck, or balcony—should not preclude a home-owner from the pleasure of growing bulbs, even if the selection is limited.

Pests and Diseases

Bulbs should be free of pests and diseases when purchased. Bulbs grown poorly, with no atten-tion to correct and timely cultural practices, will not maintain their vigor. Even with good culture, pests can be expected—aphids, slugs, and snails.

Many products are available to control pests and diseases. Whenever possible, spraying should be the last resort in any control program. Elimination of pests by washing plants with water and the use of soaps and biological controls should always take precedence over the use of chemicals. Should a pest or disease threaten to wipe out a planting, the alternatives are stark: spray or lose the plants being attacked. The gar-dener must make a choice.

Always read the entire label of any product for specific application information, and follow the directions to the letter. If there is any doubt re-garding the appropriateness of a product, obtain further information from a fully qualified person, such as your county agricultural commissioner, extension agent, licensed pest-control operator, or a member of the staff of your local nursery.

Aphids

Aphids are sucking insects that weaken plants by disrupting the necessary flow of food inside the plant. This can cause distortion, stunting, and loss of vigor. Leaves often will yellow when the attack is severe. A jet of clean water will dislodge the pests from the foliage. Ladybugs will help con-trol minor infestations, but insecticides will be needed for severe attacks.

Borers

The European corn borer (*Ostinia nubilalis*) over-winters in corn stalks and attacks other plants, such as dahlias and gladiolus. The caterpillar emerges in late summer or early spring. The larva is light pink, while the egg-laying female moth is yellow-brown and mostly nocturnal. Cleanliness is one of the best controls, but, should the cater-pillar be found, the affected plants should be at once discarded.

Stalk borer (*Papaipema nebris*) can be found on many summer-flowering bulbs east of the Rocky Mountains in the United States. The cater-pillar is pale yellow with a purplish band. Spray with a product to eradicate.

Nematodes

Seldom visible to the naked eye, nematodes are abundant in most soils. Not all are harmful, how-ever, some being responsible for the breakdown of organic matter in the soil. They are one of the main pests responsible for root decay, which in turn can cause deformed foliage, even causing the leaves to split and bulbs to have much browned tissue. Remove the bulb with a sample of the surrounding soil and have both examined by the local authority.

Bulb Flies

Narcissus fly attacks *Narcissus* and sometimes *Amaryllis*, *Galanthus*, and *Leucojum*. The adult lays eggs in the neck of the bulb when the fo-liage dies down. The larvae eat the bulb under-ground, destroying the center. Any foliage will be at best very weak and yellow. Control of this pests involves keeping the surface of the soil dis-turbed as the foliage dies, covering the hole lead-ing to the neck of the bulbs. Any bulbs attacked should be destroyed. The soil can be dusted with a product recommended and listed as a control.

Whiteflies are seldom noticed unless in large numbers. The wings are covered with a powdery substance which gives them both their color and their common name. *Trialeurodes* is the most common genus. Adult females lay light yellow eggs on the undersides of leaves. After the eggs hatch, the nymphs feed by piercing the leaf to obtain its sap. The plants are weakened as the sap is removed; foliage turns yellow and dries up. When plants are infested, a chemical product should be used.

Mealybug

Mealybugs are most common on bulbous plants with persistent evergreen foliage, such as *Clivia*. The name was given because of the waxy, white, mealy secretions that cover their bodies. Mealybugs are found on young foliage, where they feed by drawing sap, which causes distortion of the shoots in severe cases. To clear away small infestations, apply denatured alcohol to the pests with a cotton swab. Use an insecticide in severe cases.

Thrips

The gladiolus thrip (*Taeniothrips simplex*) and the onion thrip (*Thrips tabaci*) are particularly troublesome. The latter will attack dahlias, gloxinias, and other garden flowers. Thrips shave off the outer layers of the leaves to feed on the sap-containing tissues. This causes strips of yellow-to-brown foliage, and, on gladiolus leaves, a silvery appearance. Flowers, if produced, are distorted. The onion thrip causes white blotches on the leaves. The tips then turn brown and distorted. Eventually, the whole plant will topple. As with most pests, thrips are kept at a minimum by the use of clean cultural procedures, including the eradication of weeds.

Mites

Only a few mites attack bulbs. The spider mites, often called red spiders, actually can be green, yellow, or brown, as well as red. In warmer climates they attack early spring-flowering bulbs, and in colder climates where the temperatures rise more quickly in the spring, they affect a wide range of bulbs. The mites suck the nutrients from the leaves, which turn dry and yellowish. Webs can be seen on the leaf underside. Hosing the foliage with a sharp jet of cold water may reduce the population, but spraying with an in-

secticide is more effective. Cyclamen mite, like the spider mite, flourishes during the dry summer months.

Slugs and Snails

Clean cultivation assists greatly in reducing the number of slugs and snails, but, as a precaution, suitable baits should be used as the bulbs emerge from the ground. Picking these pests off the plants by hand when they emerge in the evening is the most effective control. A dusting of diatomaceous earth may be needed in more serious attacks.

Botrytis

During cool, damp summers of temperate climates and in cooler winters of subtropical climates, small yellow or orange-brown spots may be noticed on the leaves. In a short time the spots become larger, until the entire leaf or surface of the bulb is covered and a gray mold becomes evident. Bulbs showing any signs of these spots should never be planted. Fungicides will control the fungus.

Damping-off Disease

Damping-off (*Pythium debaryanum*) is a soil-borne disease that attacks young seedlings just at soil level, causing the stems to become pinched and to often turn black as the tissue dies. The disease is encouraged by lack of air circulation and excessive dampness. The best control is to use sterilized soil, thin seedlings as soon as they are large enough to handle, and keep seedlings growing well, with just the right amount of water. Discard plants attacked, along with any infected soil, and meticulously clean all containers.

Mildew

Downy mildew looks like cotton and is most prevalent when the temperature is low and humidity high. Numerous effective controls are available.

Powdery mildew (*Erysiphe* species) is common on the West Coast of the United States. The spores are spread by the wind and can be particularly bothersome in shaded areas. The fungus is first seen on the undersides of older leaves as small, white spots, followed by a weblike appearance that spreads to cover the entire underside of the leaf. When the attack is severe, the leaf yellows, then browns, and thus is useless to plant. Certain fungicides will control this disease, but more than one application generally is necessary.

Verticillium Wilt

Verticillium wilt (*Verticillium albo-atrum*) lives in the soil and enters the plant through the roots. It causes the vascular system to malfunction; the plant slowly dwindles away and dies. Verticillium also can be the cause of plants wilting under stress. Although these plants will recover in the cool of the evening, the wilting gradually increases and finally the entire plant wilts and dies. Control involves fumigating the soil and rotating plants regularly.

Virus

All plants are susceptible to virus. In tulips the symptoms are the "breaking" or mottling of the colors in the flowers; in lilies the plants are weak and flowers often aborted. The foliage is mottled and, when held up to the light, irregular streaking is seen. All parts of the plants are best lifted and discarded. Virus diseases are spread by aphids and other sucking insects.

BULBS FOR SPECIFIC PURPOSES AND LOCATIONS

The lists that follow are representative only and do not include every bulb described in this guide. Gardeners are encouraged to be creative in their use of bulbs in the landscape.

Blue Flowers

Agapanthus
Allium giganteum
Anemone blanda
Brimeura amethystina
Camassia quamash
Chiondoxa sardensis
Crocus chrysanthus 'Blue Pearl'
Crocus kotschyanus
Freesia 'Royal Blue'
Hyacinthoides italica
Ipheion uniflorum 'Wisley Blue'
Muscari azureum
Scilla

Purple Flowers

Achimenes longiflora 'Paul Arnold'
Allium carinatum
Anemone nemorosa 'Robinsoniana'
Colchicum autumnale 'Nancy Lindsay'
Corydalis solida
Crocus cartwrightianus
Cyclamen pseudibericum
Fritillaria persica 'Adiyaman'
Iris japonica
Muscari armeniacum
Sparaxis grandiflora
Tulipa 'Negrita'

Pink Flowers

Allium unifolium
Amaryllis belladonna
Colchicum byzantinum
Cyclamen coum
Dicentra spectabilis
Eremurus robustus
Erythronium dens-canis
Freesia 'Adonis'
Hippeastrum 'Apple Blossom'
Hyacinthus orientalis 'Pink Pearl'

Nerine bowdenii
Schizostylis coccinea 'Sunrise'

Red Flowers

Anemone blanda 'Radar'
Canna 'Roi Humbert'
Crocosmia 'Lucifer'
Hemerocallis 'Bald Eagle'
Lilium chalcedonicum
Scadoxus multiflorus subsp. *katherinae*
Schizostylis coccinea var. *major*
Trillium erectum
Tulipa 'Oxford'
Tulipa 'Red Emperor'
Veltheimia bracteata

Orange Flowers

Begonia boliviensis 'Firecracker'
Canna 'Phaison'
Canna 'Wyoming'
Clivia miniata
Crocosmia
Hyacinthus orientalis 'Gipsy Queen'
Lachenalia aloides var. *aurea*
Lilium 'Orange Pixie'
Tritonia crocata
Tropaeolum tuberosum 'Ken Aslet'
Watsonia zeyheri

Yellow Flowers

Allium moly 'Jeannine'
Begonia 'Primrose'
Bloomeria crocea
Calochortus luteus
Canna 'Richard Wallace'
Clivia miniata 'Citrina'
Crocus chrysanthus
Eranthis hyemalis
Eremurus stenophyllus
Freesia 'Wintergold'

Opposite: Spikes of *Eucomis* (foreground) with mountain cabbage tree, *Cussonia paniculata* (background) (Jack Hobbs)

Fritillaria imperialis 'Lutea Maxima'
Hemerocallis 'Stella d'Oro'
Hyacinthus orientalis 'City of Haarlem'
Iris bucharica
Lilium 'Adelina'
Lilium 'Quickstep'
Narcissus cyclamineus
Ornithogalum dubium
Tulipa 'Golden Emperor'
Tulipa 'Westpoint'
Zantedeschia elliotiana

Green Flowers

Eucomis autumnalis
Ferraria crispa
Fritillaria pallidiflora

White Flowers

Allium karataviense
Anemone blanda 'White Splendor'
Cardiocrinum giganteum
Colchicum speciosum 'Album'
Convallaria majalis
Crinum ×*powellii*
Crocus chrysanthus 'Ladykiller'
Cyclamen hederifolium
Erythronium californicum 'White Beauty'
Freesia 'Matterhorn'
Galanthus
Galtonia candicans
Hyacinthus orientalis 'L'Innocence'
Leucojum vernuum
Lilium candidum
Lilium longiflorum
Nerine sarniensis
Ornithogalum thyrsoides
Polianthes tuberosa
Ranunculus acontifolius
Rhodohypoxis baurii
Trillum grandiflorum
Tulipa 'Purissima'
Zantedeschia aethiopica

Multicolored Flowers

Crocus sieberi f. *tricolor*
Dahlia hybrids
Dietes bicolor
Erythronium tuolumnense
Freesia 'Stockholm'
Gladiolus 'Candy Stripe'
Gloriosa superba 'Rothschildiana'

Hemerocallis hybrids
Hippeastrum 'Masai'
Iris versicolor
Lilium martagon
Moraea tricolor
Narcissus poeticus var. *recurvus*
Sparaxis tricolor
Tulipa 'Kees Nelis'
Tulipa 'Plaisir'

Colored Foliage

Arum italicum 'Pictum'
Caladium hybrids
Canna 'Phaison'
Iris pseudacorus 'Variegata'

Early Spring Flowers

Anemone
Arisaema ringens
Chiondoxa
Crocus biflorus
Cyclamen persicum
Dietes bicolor
Eranthis hyemalis
Fritillaria imperialis
Iris bucharica
Lachenalia aloides
Leucojum vernum
Muscari neglectum
Narcissus cyclamineus
Narcissus minor
Ornithogalum oligophyllum
Oxalis lutea
Puschkinia scilloides
Scilla miczenkoana
Trillium
Tulipa fosteriana
Veltheimia bracteata

Spring Flowers

Babiana
Brimeura amethystina
Camassia quamash
Corydalis solida
Erythronium
Freesia leichtlinii
Hyacinthus orientalis
Ixia
Lapeirousia
Muscari
Narcissus

Ranunculus acontifolius
Romulea
Sparaxis elegans
Tulbaghia violacea
Tulipa greigii
Watsonia borbonica
Zantedeschia

Late Spring Flowers

Arum italicum
Bloomeria crocea
Boophone disticha
Bulbinella cauda-felis
Calochortus
Chasmanthe floribunda
Convallaria majalis
Dicentra spectabilis
Dierama pendulum
Eremurus himalaicus
Ferraria crispa
Geranium tuberosum 'Leonidas'
Gladiolus communis
Homeria pallida
Iris pallida
Iris pseudacorus
Ixiolirion tataricum
Muscari latifolium
Narcissus poeticus
Ornithogalum nutans
Scilla peruviana
Trillium grandiflorum
Triteleia ixioides
Tulipa clusiana

Early Summer Flowers

Bloomeria crocea
Boophone disticha
Dicentra spectabilis
Dierama
Ferraria crispa
Ixiolirion tataricum
Kniphofia uvaria
Leucocoryne ixioides
Sauromatum venosum

Summer Flowers

Agapanthus
Alstroemeria
Belamcanda chinensis
Dracunculus
Eucomis

Galtonia candicans
Gloriosa superba
Iris
Nectaroscordum siculum
Polianthes tuberosa
Sandersonia aurantiaca
Scadoxus multiflorus
Sparaxis elegans
Tigridia
Trillium
Tulipa
Watsonia borbonica
Zantedeschia

Late Summer Flowers

Achimenes longiflora 'Paul Arnold'
Amaryllis belladonna
Begonia
Canna
Cardiocrinum giganteum
Crinum
Lycoris
Pancratium maritimum
Schizostylis coccinea

Autumn Flowers

Begonia
Colchicum
Crinum americanum
Crocus biflorus
Crocus laevigatus
Cyclamen hederifolium
Cyrtanthus
Lycoris ×*albiflora*
Nerine
Schizostylis coccinea
Sternbergia

Winter Flowers in Cold Climates

Anemone blanda
Chiondoxa
Crocus chrysanthus
Crocus laevigatus
Cyclamen coum
Cyclamen persicum
Eranthis
Freesia
Galanthus nivalis
Iris danfordiae
Iris unguicularis
Leucojum vernum

Winter Flowers in Warm Climates

Bulbinella
Clivia miniata
Eucharis ×*grandiflora*
Ipheion uniflorum
Moraea tricolor
Oxalis purpurea
Romulea
Scilla miczenkoana
Veltheimia bracteata

Bulbs for Forcing

Allium neapolitanum
Amaryllis belladonna
Anemone coronaria
Crocus vernus
Hyacinthus orientalis
Narcissus
Trillium
Tulipa

Bulbs for Shade and Woodland

The obvious differences between locations with cool temperatures but bright sunshine and those with high temperatures and bright sunshine make it difficult to produce a list which indicates the exact shade required by various genera. A plant may well take full sun along the cooler areas of a coastline but is unable to withstand full sun in much warmer inland areas. In the listing of genera that follows, readers should use their local knowledge, dependent on their exact location, to determine the amount of shade a plant needs.

All woodlands have areas which are shaded for a number of hours a day but also receive intervals of bright sunlight. Few bulbs appreciate being grown entirely in the shade; most prefer at least short periods of brighter light.

Anemone
Arisaema
Arum
Begonia
Caladium
Cardiocrinum giganteum
Clivia
Corydalis solida
Cyclamen

Dicentra spectabilis
Dracunculus vulgaris
Erythronium
Galanthus
Hyacinthoides
Lachenalia aloides
Muscari
Scadoxus multiflorus
Trillium
Veltheimia bracteata

Cut Flowers

Agapanthus
Allium
Alstroemeria
Amaryllis belladonna
Anemone De Caen Group
Anemone St. Brigid Group
Babiana stricta
Belamcanda chinensis
Chasmanthe floribunda
Clivia
Crinum
Crocosmia
Cyclamen
Dahlia
Dierama pendulum
Eremurus stenophyllus
Eucharis ×*grandiflora*
Eucomis autumnalis
Freesia
Galanthus
Galtonia candicans
Gladiolus
Gloriosa superba
Hippeastrum
Iris
Ixia
Lilium
Narcissus
Nerine
Ornithogalum thyrsoides
Polianthes tuberosa
Ranunculus
Sparaxis
Tulipa
Veltheimia bracteata
Watsonia
Zantedeschia

Fragrant Flowers

Cardiocrinum giganteum
Crinum ×powellii
Crocus sieberi
Cyclamen pseudibericum
Cyrtanthus mackenii
Eucharis ×grandiflora
Freesia leichtlinii
Galanthus
Gladiolus
Hemerocallis
Hyacinthus
Ipheion uniflorum
Iris
Leucocoryne ixioides
Leucojum vernum
Lilium
Lycoris incarnata
Muscari armeniacum
Muscari macrocarpum
Narcissus ×odorus
Pancratium maritimum
Polianthes tuberosa
Tulbaghia violacea
Tulipa saxatilis

Bulbs for Rock Gardens

Allium flavum
Bloomeria crocea
Brimeura amethystina
Chionodoxa
Colchicum
Corydalis solida
Cyclamen
Ferraria crispa
Fritillaria
Iris bucharica
Iris reticulata
Ixiolirion tataricum
Lapeirousia
Narcissus
Ornithogalum
Puschkinia scilloides
Ranunculus acontifolius
Rhodohypoxis
Romulea
Scilla
Tritonia
Tulipa

Overleaf: *Freesia* hybrid (Jack Hobbs)

Achimenes longiflora

Panama to Mexico. Rhizomes pear-shaped, scaly, white, 2–3 in. (5–7.5 cm) long. Stems to 1 ft. (30 cm). Leaves coarsely toothed, arranged in whorls of three four. Flowers numerous, usually pale to dark blue, sometimes pinkish, lavender or white; throat usually white, sometimes with spot of yellow or violet; borne in leaf axils; corolla tube narrow, flaring out to a flattened outer blossom 1–2½ in. (2.5–6.5 cm) across, with five lobes and four anthers.

Blooms late summer.

Sandy soil with equal parts planting mix, sharp sand, and peat moss; outdoors in filtered sunlight or light shade, indoors under artificial light 14–16 hours per day; moisture when growing. Zones 10–12.

Plant in spring, with 1 in. (2.5 cm) soil covering the rhizome.

Use as a house plant or in a cool greenhouse. Perfect for hanging baskets with its delicate colors and lush foliage.

'**Paul Arnold**', dark purple with white throat, red dots in throat.

AGAPANTHUS
Lily-of-the-Nile

A genus of 10 species from southern Africa. One of the first African genera to enter Western gardens. *Agapanthus* has a rhizome and fleshy leaf bases. The deciduous species are hardier than the evergreens. The leaves are glossy, straplike, linear, and arching. Most species are large, reaching to about 3 ft. (90 cm), but dwarf selections are available. The flowers, carried on strong stalks in a many-flowered umbel, are blue, lavender, or white, and range from tubular to openly bell-shaped. The blossoms are long-lasting.

Blooms summer.

Leafy, well-drained soil best but average soil acceptable, in full sun, moisture when growing (drought tolerant when established), allow plants

Achimenes longiflora 'Paul Arnold' (International Flower Bulb Center)

to become dry between waterings. Looks well alongside a stream or pond, but the plant itself should be above the water level. Do not over fertilize. Zones 9–11.

Plant evergreen species in fall, with the green portion of the shoot slightly above soil level, 18–24 in. 30–60 cm) apart.

Use in a border for its substantial foliage and for its blue flowers which are an ideal foil for red and yellow flowers. Can be grown in containers. A mainstay in public areas, including road medians, in Mediterranean climates. Cut flowers last well in water, and dried flowerheads are also used in arrangements.

Agapanthus africanus. African lily, blue African lily. South Africa. Stems to 2 ft. (60 cm). Leaves 18–36 in. (45–90 cm) long, evergreen. Flowers deep blue; mid summer to early fall. **Var.** *atrocaeruleus*, dark violet. Prefers acid, sandy soil and a gravel mulch.

Agapanthus africanus
in the wild

Agapanthus 'Peter Pan'

Agapanthus praecox
subsp. *orientalis*,
white-flowered form

Agapanthus 'Peter Pan', a dwarf with blue flowers.

Agapanthus praecox. South Africa. Stems to 5 ft. (1.5 m). Leaves to 3 ft. (90 cm) long, 3 in. (7.5 cm) wide, evergreen. Often sold under *A. orientalis*, *A. africanus*, or *A. umbellatus*. Cultivars may have variegated foliage.

ALLIUM
Flowering garlic, onions

A genus of 500 to 750 species in the Northern Hemisphere. The bulbs vary in size when full grown; all are fleshy and similar to the culinary onion. Some are smooth and shiny but, when cut, display the typical "onion rings." The plants have the distinctive onion smell in both foliage and bulb. The leaves may be cylindrical and hollow, or flattened. The flowers are individually small but usually numerous, forming an attractive umbel which can reach considerable size. The flowers have six tepals which are free or slightly joined at the base. The seeds are dark and angular.

Bloom depends on species.

Well-drained, humus-rich soil, more moisture in summer. Hardiness varies by species.

Plant in spring, at or above soil level.

Use large-flowered species and hybrids as accents among annuals or in the perennial border. Few alliums have ornamental foliage, so they can be placed where they will grow up among denser plants. Good cut flowers.

Allium aflatunense. Central Asia. Stems 30–36 in. (75–90 cm) tall. Leaves 1–4 in. (2.5–10 cm) across. Flowers in dense, spherical umbel, purple lilac; late spring to early summer. Plants in commerce under this name are mostly forms known only in cultivation and sometimes called *A. hollandicum*. Zones 8–10.

Allium caeruleum. Siberia, Turkestan. Stems to 2 ft. (60 cm). Leaves linear, 10–18 in. (25–45 cm) long. Flowers deep blue; mid summer. Zones 6–9.

Allium carinatum. Keeled garlic. Europe, Turkey. Stems 1–2 ft. (30–60 cm). Flowers purple, summer. Produces bulbils mixed with flowers.

Allium giganteum (Jack Hobbs)

Allium giganteum, detail (Jack Hobbs)

Allium karataviense
(International Flower
Bulb Center)

Allium moly

Very invasive. **Subsp.** *pulchellum*, the most commonly grown form, has soft rose-lavender flowers; the outer flowers are pendent, forming an elegant cascade (or fireworks) effect. One of the most pleasing alliums to grow (Davies 1992). Self-sows readily. Zones 7–10.

Allium cristophii. Star of Persia. Turkestan. Stems to 2 ft. (60 cm). Leaves three to seven, strap-shaped, 1 in. (2.5 cm) wide, 20 in. (50 cm) long. Flowers purple to metallic blue; early sum-

mer. Produces some of largest heads of any *Allium*, often 10–12 in. (25–30 cm) across. Good cut flower. Zones 7–10.

Allium flavum. Europe to Turkey. Stems 3–12 in. (7.5–30 cm). Flowers bell-shaped, glistening yellow, mid summer. A good rock garden plant. Zones 7–10. **Var.** *minus*, dwarf, flowers bright yellow, spring. **Subsp.** *tauricum*, flowers pale yellow or nearly white and tinted green, brown, or pink, filaments purplish toward the tips.

Allium neapolitanum (International Flower Bulb Center)

Allium roseum

Allium giganteum. Giant garlic. Central Asia. One of the most spectacular alliums. Stems to 4 ft. (1.2 m). Leaves 2 in. (5 cm) wide and 30 in. (75 cm) or longer. Flowers in very large heads, lilac blue; summer. An excellent bedding plant. Flowerheads often used in dry arrangements. Zones 7–9.

Allium karataviense. Central Asia. Stems to 6 in. (15 cm). Leaves 4–6 in. (10–15 cm) wide, glaucous blue, lying nearly flat on the ground; the most attractive foliage in the genus. Flowers white with hint of rose; early summer. Zones 7–9.

Allium moly. Golden garlic, yellow onion, lily leek. Spain, France. Stems to 1 ft. (30 cm). Leaves metallic blue-green, flat, 2 in. (5 cm) wide. Flowers bright yellow, on long pedicels; mid summer. Zones 7–9. 'Jeannine', robust. Excellent for naturalizing and cutting.

Allium neapolitanum. Daffodil garlic, flowering onion, Naples garlic. Europe, Turkey, North Africa. One of the finest white flowers and lack of strong onion aroma. Strong stems to 2 ft. (60 cm). Flowers cup-shaped, pure white, in loose umbels; individual florets up to 1 in. (2.5 cm) across, up to 30 per umbel. Stamens prominent,

shorter than the tepals. Leaves strap-shaped, ¾ in. (2 cm) wide, 12–18 in. (30–45 cm) long. An excellent pot plant that can be forced like narcissus. Zones 8–10. 'Grandiflorum', larger than the type.

Allium oreophilum. Central Asia. Stems 4–6 in. (10–15 cm) tall. Flowers carmine-pink; mid summer. Zones 7–9.

Allium roseum. Rosy garlic. Mediterranean region. Stems 6–22 in. (15–55 cm). Flowers bright pink; spring. No bulbils. Zones 5–9. **Var. bulbiferum**, flowers pink or white, bulbils numerous. Zones 5–9.

Allium schubertii. Eastern Mediterranean region. Stems 1–2 ft. (30–60 cm). Leaves distinctive in rose pink variety—wavy and 1 in. (2.5 cm) wide. Flowers white, silvery lavender, or rose; summer. Zones 8–10.

Allium sphaerocephalum. Round-headed leek. Eurasia. Stems to 3 ft. (90 cm). Leaves cylindrical, hollow, 2 ft. (60 cm) long. Flowers purplish or pink, in very dense raceme; early to mid summer. Zones 5–9.

Allium triquetrum. Three-cornered leek. Europe. Stems to 18 in. (45 cm), unique in *Allium* in being three-sided. Leaves basal, linear, dark

Allium triquetrum

green, 10–15 in. (25–37.5 cm) long, to 1½ in. (4 cm) wide. Flowers white with green median stripes, attractive; late spring. Partial shade. Has become a rampant weed in parts of the United States, especially where mechanical cultivation spreads the bulbs. Zones 8–10.

Allium unifolium. United States. Rhizomes short. Stems 8–24 in. (20–60 cm). Flowers pale to bright pink; late spring. Zones 8–10.

ALSTROEMERIA
Lily-of-the-Incas, Peruvian lily

A genus of at least 50 species in South America. Long known in cultivation. Many hybrids have been developed for the cutflower industry and feature dense inflorescences, bright colors (in the popular pink range), and stiff, upright stems to 2 ft. (60 cm) or more; many of these are not very cold hardy, having been selected for greenhouse cultivation. The thin, linear to lance-shaped leaves are 2–4 in. (5–10 cm) long. The flowers are usually borne in corymbs and are nontubular and brightly colored.

Blooms mid summer.

Any well-drained soil, in full sun (in very hot climates, some shade is necessary to preserve the pastel colors of hybrids), adequate moisture when growing. Zones 9–10.

Plant 8 in. (20 cm) deep, 1 ft. (30 cm) apart.

Use for cut flowers and container plants.

Alstroemeria aurea. Chile and Argentina. Stems to 3 ft. (90 cm) or more in well-grown, established plantings; high-elevation populations shorter-growing. Leaves on flowering stem 3–4 in. (7.5–10 cm) long, lanceolate, gray-green beneath. Flowers numerous, as many as 50 per stem, to 1½ in. (4 cm) in diameter. Outer petals blunt, orange tinged red, with green tips; inner petals pointed, deep orange to yellow, streaked red. Many cultivars, especially for the cutflower trade, in a wide color range: **'Lutea'**, yellow. **'Orange King'**, orange-yellow with brown spots.

Alstroemeria ligtu. Saint Martin's flower. Chile, Argentina. Stems to 2 ft. (60 cm). Leaves thin, narrowly linear to lance-shaped, 3 in. (7.5

Alstroemeria aurea
(International Flower
Bulb Center)

Alstroemeria aurea 'Orange
King' (International Flower
Bulb Center)

Alstroemeria ligtu

cm) long. Flowers in groups of two or three on each ray of the umbel; outer segments pale lilac, reddish, or white; inner segments usually yellow marked with purple; summer.

Alstroemeria pelegrina. Herb lily, Inca lily. Chile. Stems 12–14 in. (30–35 cm). Leaves lance-shaped, up to 2 in. (5 cm) long. Flowers from rose to lilac to yellow.

Alstroemeria pulchella. Brazilian parrot lily, parrot lily. Brazil. Stems 18–24 in. (45–60 cm). Flowers bright red with green tips and chocolate-brown streaks and flecks; summer.

Amaryllis belladonna
August lily, naked lady

South Africa. Bulbs brown, large, and rounded, poisonous to humans and livestock, causing respiratory paralysis if eaten. Stems to 30 in. (75 cm). Leaves erect, straplike, green throughout winter in milder climates, then dying down. Flowers borne in an umbel of up to 10 on short stalks, large, sweet-scented, broadly funnel-shaped, white to deep pink, appearing before the leaves.

Blooms late summer.

Sandy, humus-rich soil, in full sun (except in hot, arid regions, where it appreciates some shade). Give moisture in fall and spring, keep dry in sum-

mer after the bulbs die down If summer moisture is abundant, shelter bulbs with sheet of glass or plastic but allow free access of air. Begin watering as soon as the flower spike appears. Top-dress with 10–10–10 fertilizer as the flowers begin to fade and the foliage emerges. Zones 8–10.

Plant in late spring with the necks just at soil level. Where winter temperatures fall below freezing, plant the bulbs 5 or 6 in. (12.5–15 cm) deep. Where winter temperatures reach 10°F (–12°C), plant deep and protect with a light-weight mulch at least 3 in. (7.5 cm) deep.

Use among low-growing shrubs, provided dry conditions exist there during summer. Excellent cut flowers. Often forced for Christmas. Though they grow well in containers, they are uninteresting in summer.

Var. *blanda*, large white.

'Bloemfontein', pale pink.

'Cape Town', deep rose red.

'Jagersfontein', deep pink.

'Johannesburg', pale pink with lighter throat.

'Kewensis', pink with yellow throat.

'Kimberley', deep carmine red with white center.

'Major', dark stems and dark pink flowers.

'Port Elizabeth' (syn. 'Beacon'), crimson.

'Purpurea', purple-rose.

Amaryllis belladonna (Jack Hobbs)

Amaryllis 'Port Elizabeth' (Jack Hobbs)

'Rosea', white stripes on rose tepals.

'Windhoek', lovely rose pink with white center.

AMORPHOPHALLUS
Devil's tongue, snake palm

A genus of about 90 species from the Old World tropics, subtropics, and Australia, some with gigantic and dramatic inflorescences and extremely large cormous or tuberous rootstocks. A solitary leaf, which in some species is more than 10 ft. (3 m) across, is produced after the flowers; the leaf may bear cormlets above ground. The spathe (the "hood" of the inflorescence) is rolled together, with wavy edges, and its lower portion may overlap; spathes are dark purple-red, dull green, or whitish pink, paler inside. The spadix, often gigantic and with an unpleasant odor, is dirty yellow. Male flowers are borne on the upper part of the spadix, female below, with no sterile flowers intervening.

Blooms spring.

Very loose, humus-rich soil, in sun or bright shade; abundant moisture, high humidity, and regular feedings when growing. Zone 11.

Plant 3–5 in. (7.5–12.5 cm) deep.

Use for warm and subtropical areas, warm greenhouse borders, and large containers. The plants are striking. The foul smell of the flowers may deter all but the dedicated aroid collector.

Amorphophallus bulbifer. Snake's tongue. Myanmar, India. Tuber to 3 in. (7.5 cm) across. Leaf stalk to 3 ft. (90 cm), olive green with paler spots. Leaf blade about 3 ft. (90 cm) wide, divided into three sections, often with cormlets produced at the junctions of the ribs. Spathe 4–6 in. (10–15 cm) long, green, spotted rose on the exterior and reddish at the base, rose to red exterior; stem of inflorescence brown with grayish spots. Spadix pink and greenish.

Amorphophallus konjac (syns. *A. mairei*, *A. rivieri*). Devil's tongue, snake palm, umbrella

Amorphophallus konjac (center) with *Hosta montana* (lower right) and *Polygonatum odoratum* 'Variegatum' (lower left) (W. George Schmid)

Amorphophallus konjac, stem coloration (W. George Schmid)

arum. Indonesia. Corm flattish, to 10 in. (25 cm) across, edible. Leaf stalk to 3 ft. (90 cm), brownish green spotted white. Leaf blade much branched, 3 ft. (90 cm) or more wide. Flower stem 24–30 in. (60–75 cm) long. Spathe 18 in. (45 cm) long, basal tube green spotted greenish white; as it flattens, it becomes dark purple on the inside, green outside. Spadix as much as 8 in. (20 cm) longer than the spathe, dark red-brown. Grown for food. Reportedly frost-hardy if well mulched.

Amorphophallus paeoniifolius. Elephant yam, Telingo potato. India, New Guinea, Asia, Australasia. Corm 8–10 in. (20–25 cm) thick, flattened, edible. Leaf generally solitary, sometimes two. Leaf stalk often warty, 20–30 in. (50–75 cm), dark green with paler spots. Leaf blade to 2 ft. (60 cm) wide and long, divided into 3 lobes, the outer finely cut. Flower stem to 10 in. (25 cm). Spathe 8 in. (20 cm) long and 10 in.

(25 cm) wide, green outside, spotted white inside, purplish at base, the broader portion green to purple with a wavy margin. Spadix 1 ft. (30 cm) long, with appendix 6 in. (15 cm) long, spongy, deep purple.

ANEMONE
Windflower, lily-of-the-field

A genus of about 120 species in the Northern and Southern Hemispheres. Only a few are tuberous or rhizomatous. The foliage of most is lobed to finely divided; many species have a whorl of leaves on the stalk just below the flowers. The colorful floral segments are actually petal-like sepals. The genus offers a full range of colors: white, yellow, red, pink, blue, and violet.

Blooms early spring.

Sandy, humus-rich soil, preferably leafmold, shade in spring and summer, moisture when growing but not wet soil. Hardiness varies by species.

Plant in early fall, 1–1½ in. (2.5–4 cm) deep, 6–8 in. (15–20 cm) apart. Lay tuber on its side if root is not apparent.

Use in masses. Among the best early flowering plants for the woodland, where they can be allowed to naturalize. Plant these low growers where they can be appreciated—perhaps on a shady bank beneath high-crowned trees—but away from paths where dormant plants may be trampled. Both Saint Brigid and De Caen Groups are excellent cut flowers, garden, and container plants.

Anemone blanda (Jack Hobbs)

Anemone apennina. Southern Europe. Similar to *A. blanda* but larger, and stems smooth rather than hairy. Rhizome thick, almost tuberous, elongated, very dark. Stems to 6 in. (15 cm). Flowers solitary, pale to deep blue; late winter to early spring. Zone 6. **'Albiflora'**, white with tinge of light blue on reverse. **'Petrovac'**, robust deep blue.

Anemone blanda. Southeastern Europe. Tubers rounded, lumpy, dark. Stems to 6 in. (15 cm). Flowers solitary, usually deep blue, but pale blue, white, and pink forms occur; late winter to early spring. Zones 5–9. **'Alba'**, white, plant slightly smaller than type, flowers a little larger. **'Blue Shades'**, light blue. **'Bridesmaid'**, large pure white. **'Charmer'**, deep pink. **'Pink Star'**, large deep pink. **'Radar'**, showy bright red with white center. **'Rosea'**, clear pink. **'Violet Star'**, red-violet. **'White Splendour'**, very large, pure white, long-lasting flowers.

Anemone blanda 'Bridesmaid'

Anemone coronaria. Poppy anemone. Mediterranean region. Tubers knobby, brown. Stems 8–12 in. (20–30 cm). Flowers solitary, scarlet, white, blue, pink, or bicolored. Plant in late fall for spring flowering, early spring for mid summer flowering, late spring for late summer to early fall flowering. Responds well to gentle forcing. Popular cut flower. Zones 8–10. The **De Caen Group** of poppy-flowered singles includes **'His Excellency'**, bright scarlet, very large, on good stems; **'Mister Fokker'**, blue; and **'The Bride'**, pure white. The double to semidouble **Saint Brigid Group** includes **'Lord Lieutenant'**,

Anemone blanda 'White Splendor' with *Tulipa* 'Twinkle'

Anemone coronaria (Jack Hobbs)

Anemone coronaria De Caen Group (Jack Hobbs)

Anemone coronaria Saint Brigid Group

Anemone nemorosa

Anemone nemorosa 'Flore Pleno'

bright blue; **'Mount Everest'**, white; and **'The Admiral'**, cyclamen-violet.

Anemone nemorosa. Wood anemone. Europe. Stems 6–8 in. (15–20 cm). Flowers white, often tinged pink on the exterior, 1 in. (2.5 cm) across; early to mid spring. Zones 5–9. **'Alba Plena'**, double white with a pompon of tiny petals in the center. **'Allenii'**, rose lilac on outside, light blue inside. **'Flore Pleno'**, double. **'Leeds' Variety'**, large single white. **'Robinsoniana'**, delicate lavender-blue, foliage deep green tinged purple, low-growing. **'Royal**

Anemone ranunculoides

characteristics. The seeds are enclosed in a fleshy fruit which, in most species, turns brilliant orange when ripe.

Well-drained, humus-rich soil, in filtered sunlight, moisture when growing, dry in winter. Hardiness varies by species.

Plant in fall or spring, 3–4 in. (7.5–10 cm) deep, 10–12 in. (25–30 cm) apart. Some growers like to plant the tubers 12 in. (30 cm) deep for winter protection in colder climates.

Use in woodlands, especially along streams, where there is adequate moisture and much organic matter in the soil. The plants' greatest merit is in their foliage, growing among other foliage plants, such as *Hosta*, *Rodgersia*, and ferns, which also like moisture and shade. They are well adapted to the eastern United States, where they enjoy the summer rain and humidity; in the western states, place them in regularly irrigated sites.

Arisaema anomalum. Malaya. Rootstock fleshy. Leaves and flowers appear at same time. Leaf stalk to 12 in. (30 cm); leaflets three, more or less equal, lance-shaped, 4–6 in. (10–15 cm) long. Spathe has white stripes on dark brown to greenish purple background. Late spring. Requires frost-free conditions with plenty of moisture. Zone 11.

Arisaema candidissimum. China. Tuber flattish, round. Stem 15–18 in. (37.5–45 cm). Flowers appear before leaves, in early summer. Spathe white with pinkish stripes inside; outside pale apple-green, especially at base. Spadix yellowish green. Leaf large, leaflets three. Orange seeds frequently produced in late summer. Zones 6–9.

Arisaema dracontium. Green dragon, dragon root. North America. Tuber oblong, about ¾ in. (2 cm) thick. Spadix often more than 10 in. (25 cm) long, extending from spathe; both are green, or spadix may be yellowish. Leaves 18 in. (45 cm) long, divided, slender, pointed. Flowers nestle under them on stems 18–30 in. (45–75 cm). Leaf stalk mottled white at base. Late spring to early summer. Orange-red fruits in late summer. Good for moist, shady areas. Zones 4–9.

Blue', violet-blue, tinged rose purple on reverse, very dark green foliage tinged purple, low-growing.

Anemone ranunculoides. Buttercup anemone. Europe. Rhizome slender, spreading horizontally and rapidly. Stems to 6 in. (15 cm) but often shorter. Flowers with few segments, bright yellow. Plant in full sun, except in hot regions. Zones 4–9. **Subsp.** *wockeana* is a little looser in form and smaller than the type, and the flowers are closer to the foliage.

ARISAEMA
Cobra lily

A genus of 170 species in the Himalayas, West Asia, tropical Africa, and eastern North America. Closely allied to *Arum* but distinguished by the absence of sterile flowers on the spadix. The one to three leaves are composed of leaflets. In some species the spadix bears male and female flowers on different plants, while in others it carries female flowers on the lower part and male flowers on the upper. The attractive spadix in many species has a terminal appendix, curved or whip-like and extending as much as 18 in. (45 cm). The color, form, and size of the ornamental bract (spathe) provide the most obvious identifying

Arum italicum 'Pictum' (W. George Schmid)

Arisaema propinquum (David M. Ward)

Arisaema propinquum. Himalaya. Spathe deep purple (rarely green), blade striped white, margins checkered pale green. Spadix tail-like, purple. Late spring. Zones 5–10.

Arisaema ringens. Japan, Korea, China. Tuber flattened. Spathe striped green and white or plain purplish, deeply hooded, lobes purple within; blade deep purple. Leaves appear after flowering, three-lobed, stout. Very early spring. Zones 7–10.

Arisaema tortuosum. Himalaya. Tuber flat, round, very large, up to 4 ft. (1.2 m) across! Inflorescence on short stalk before leaf emerges. Spathe green, or rarely dark purple, late spring. Leaf stalk 5–6 ft. (1.5–1.8 m). Zones 7–10.

ARUM

A genus of about 26 species from Europe (especially around the Mediterranean) and West Asia, with others in North Africa and the Himalaya. The inflorescence consists of a spikelike spadix, surrounded by a broad spathe. The spadix bears female flowers on the bottom and male flowers above, separated by a zone of sterile, rudimentary flowers. The female flowers have a one-celled ovary. The spadix has a tip where sterile flowers (or no flowers) occur. The leaves are not lobed. These two features—unlobed leaves and the male and female flowers on the spadix with sterile flowers between— distinguish *Arum* from *Arisaema*. The leaves are produced before the flowers.

Blooms in early spring.

Humus-rich soil, in sun or light shade, moisture when growing, No fertilizer is needed, but top-dressing with organic matter each year in the fall is beneficial.

Arum maculatum

Arum maculatum

Plant 3–4 in. (7.5–10 cm) deep, 8–12 in. (20–30 cm) apart.

Use in the woodland garden or in the wild garden.

Arum italicum. Mediterranean region. Rootstock a tuber. Leaves produced in fall or early winter, carried on strong stems 6–15 in. (15–37.5 cm) long. Leaf blade arrow- or heart-shaped, often veined silver-gray, cream, or yellowish green, often marked with irregular purple-black spots, seldom entirely green. Spathe 5–10 in. (12.5–25 cm), on a strong stem 4–8 in. (10–20 cm), greenish white inside, greenish to yellowish outside, base often brownish purple. Spadix 4–6 in. (10–15 cm), dark yellow. Late spring to early summer. Zones 6–10. **Subsp.** *albispathum*, spathe usually white inside and outside, spadix pale yellow. **Subsp.** *italicum* 'Cyclops', large, dark green foliage, reliable flowering. **Subsp.** *italicum* 'Spotted Jack', leaves both veined and black-spotted. **Subsp.** *neglectum*, spathe green-ish white with brown-purple stain along external margins and midvein, distinctive foliage, first leaves in early winter oval with two equal triangular lobes, followed by leaves that are narrower and more arrow-shaped.

Arum maculatum. Lords-and-ladies, cuckoopint. Europe. Leaves 12–18 in. (30–45 cm) long, often spotted purple, to 12 in. (30 cm) tall. Spathe pale yellowish green inside, deeper-colored and spotted purple outside. Spadix darker yellow. Spring. A rampant spreader and the hardiest species in the genus. Zones 6–9.

BABIANA
Baboon flower
Comprises 60–70 species from sub-Sahara Africa, where baboons dig the corms for food. Plants seldom surpass 18 in. (45 cm). The leaves are ribbed, tapered, pleated, and stiff, held in fans; both leaves and stems are more or less coated with short hairs. The flowers are brightly colored, often

Babiana disticha. Blue babiana. South Africa. Flowers blue with yellow throat, fragrant.

Babiana stricta. South Africa. Corm small, fibrous covered. Stems to 18 in. (45 cm). Leaves to 5 in. (12.5 cm) long, ½ in. (12 mm) wide. Flowers cream to crimson, lilac, or blue; tepals six, open widely to 2 in. (5 cm) across, base slightly funnel-shaped. 'Blue Gem', stems 8 in. (20 cm), flowers violet with purple flecks. Var. *grandiflora*, flowers bright blue marked with pink. 'Purple Sensation', stems 16 in. (40 cm), flowers bright purple with white markings. 'Purple Star', stems 12–13 in. (30–32.5 cm), flowers dark cyclamen-violet with white-striped throat. Var. *sulphurea*, flowers cream or pale yellow with blue anthers and yellow stigmas, mid spring. 'Tubergen's Blue', stems 12–16 in. (30–40 cm), flowers large lavender-violet with darker blotches. 'White King', stems 12–16 in. (30–40 cm), flowers white with pale blue stripes on reverse, anthers lobelia-blue. 'Zwanenburg Glory', dark lavender-violet with white blotches.

BEGONIA

A genus of more than 350 species, found in humid tropics and subtropics around the globe, especially in the Americas. Only tuberous species are described here. Many plants have luxurious growth, striking foliage, and beautiful flowers. It is possible to have begonias in flower every month of the year. The flowers can be very large, in a wide range of colors. They are unisexual; the male flower is showier than the female. The number of stamens many, and the filaments are free or united at the base. There are two to four styles, and the stigmas are either branched or twisted. The fruit is a capsule, often winged, containing many minute, dustlike seeds.

Blooms summer to fall.

Well-drained, moisture-retentive mixture of equal parts topsoil, peat moss and sand; filtered sunlight is ideal, shade in hotter climates and during the hottest part of the day in summer; never completely dry. Zones 6–9.

Babiana stricta (Jack Hobbs)

two-toned; three to many are borne on a stem that may be branched or unbranched. The six tepals open widely to a diameter of 2 in. (5 cm) and have a slightly funnel-shaped base.

Blooms early to late spring.

Sandy soil, in full sun, moisture when growing but never waterlogged. Zones 9–11.

Plant in late summer or early fall, 6 in. (15 cm) deep in average and sandy soils, 6 in. (15 cm) apart.

Use for variety and winter bloom in gardens in warm Mediterranean climates. These delightful flowers do not occupy much space; they are good container plants.

Plant in late winter, covering lightly with soil, 2–3 in. (5–7.5 cm) apart. Place tuber convex side up and even with surface of soil, concave side down.

Use tuberous begonias, in all their different forms, in containers and bedding out. Pendent types are best in an elevated position so the foliage and flowers hang over the edge of the container at or above eye level. They are very decorative in hanging baskets or containers attached to a wall.

Begonia boliviensis 'Firecracker'. Stems arching. Flowers bright orange-red, 2 in. (5 cm) long, bell-shaped.

Begonia grandis subsp. *evansiana*. Hardy begonia. Malaysia, China, Japan. Stems to 3 ft. (90 cm), branching, red, produced annually. Bulbils produced in axils of leaves. Leaves large, pointed, with heart-shaped base and shallowly lobed margins, coppery to green-red veins above, red beneath. Flowers fragrant, pendent, white or pink, a little over 1 in. (2.5 cm) across. Male flowers have four tepals of unequal length; female flowers have two tepals and ovary is distinctly pink.

Belamcanda chinensis
Blackberry lily, leopard lily

Rootstock a slender, stoloniferous rhizome. Foliage deep green and irislike, arranged in fans; the leaves encircle the branching stem, and the lower ones are longer than those above. Flowers showy, to 2 in. (5 cm) across, yellow to red-orange, always with deep red-brown spots, individually not long-lasting but produced in loose, branching heads of up to 12 blossoms. Perianth segments narrow at the base, almost flat when fully open; tube very short. Attractive, dark purple-black seeds, visible as the seed pods open, resemble blackberries.

Blooms mid to late summer.

Sandy, well-drained soil with some humus, in a warm spot, moisture when growing. Zones 8–10.

Plant in fall in warmer areas, in spring in colder areas, 1 in. (2.5 cm) deep, 6–8 in. (15–20 cm) apart.

Begonia boliviensis 'Firecracker' (Jack Hobbs)

Tuberous begonias (Jack Hobbs)

Begonia 'Primrose' (Jack Hobbs)

Belamcanda chinensis (International Flower Bulb Center)

Use for color and interest in mixed and herbaceous borders. The individual plants take up little space and can be inserted among more permanent plantings. The seed pods are unusual material for dried flower arrangements.

Bloomeria crocea

United States. Corms covered with a fibrous coat. Leaf solitary, basal, 1 ft. (30 cm) or more long, narrow. Flowers deep yellow, starry, with dark median lines on tepals; umbels 4–6 in. (10–15 cm) across; perianth segments free to the base, so flowers open flat; six stamens form a sheath around the ovary.

Blooms late spring or early summer.

Very well drained soil, in full sun, adequate moisture in winter and spring. Zones 9–11.

Plant in late summer (late spring in cold climates), 4 in. (20 cm) deep, deeper in hot, dry climates, 12 in. (30 cm) deep in hard clay.

Use for interest in perennial and shrub plantings. Will multiply if left undisturbed. Does well in rock gardens, but position plants so the tall flower stems will not overpower neighbors.

Bloomerias grow well in pots and make excellent cut flowers.

Var. *aurea*, corm the size of a hazelnut, stems 6–12 in. (15–30 cm) long, flowers particularly bright yellow.

Var. *montana*, similar to var. *aurea* but petals recurve more and flowers do not have a slight cup formed by the bases of the perianth segments.

Boophone disticha
Century plant, tumbleweed

Southern and tropical Africa. Bulbs 6 in. (15 cm) or more across, covered with dry scales; the upper two-thirds of the bulb is often above ground level. Leaves basal, linear, emerging after flowers, arranged in two ranks as a fan, to 14 in. (35 cm) long, about 2 in. (5 cm) wide, tapering, often with fluted edges. Flowers in large umbels—over 12 in. (30 cm) across—of 50 or more, on a leafless flower stalk only a few inches long. Perianth segments pink, narrow, curled and twisted but not much reflexed. Individual flowers ½ in. (12 mm) or more across, with prominent orange stamens.

Blooms late spring to early summer.

Average soil, in full sun, moisture when growing and flowering. Zones 9–11.

Plant so that the neck and about half of the bulb are above ground level, about 12 in. (30 cm) apart.

Use for its large size and long flowering period. In warm climates, suitable for the sunny border or a corner of the garden with sun and good drainage. In colder areas, can be grown in deep containers, protected over winter by moving indoors.

Brimeura amethystina

Pyrenees. Bulb elliptical, to ¾ in. (2 cm) across. Leaves six to eight, narrow, linear, bright green, to 12 in. (30 cm) long. Stems to 10 in. (25 cm). Flowers 5–15 in a one-sided, loose raceme, bright blue, bell-shaped, nearly ½ in. (12 mm) long, pendent; tepal lobes are shorter than the tube. A long, tapering bract subtends each flower.

Bloomeria crocea (Helen Crocker Russell Library, San Francisco)

Boophone disticha, flower

Boophone disticha, foliage (Jack Hobbs)

Brimeura amethystina (International Flower Bulb
Center)

Blooms in mid spring.

Well-drained soil, in full sun, moisture in growing season, dry in summer. A mulch of leaves
helps to extend their adaptability. Fertilize very little; the leafmold mulch is sufficient. Zones 9–11.

Plant in fall, 1–2 in. (2.5–5 cm) deep, 3–5 in.
(7.5–12.5 cm) apart.

Use as a low-growing bulb for a sunny border
or rock garden. Placement near rocks also seems
beneficial: they appreciate the reflected heat.
Dainty but not showy in small containers.

'Alba', white.

BULBINELLA

A genus of about 22 species, some with enlarged, erect rhizomes covered with fibers. The
leaves are linear to threadlike and basal. The
flowers are carried in a raceme, looking like a
small *Kniphofia* species, often with well over 100
flowers on a stem. The colors range from white

Bulbinella cauda-felis

to yellow-orange, and the flowers are only about ⅓ in. (8 mm) across.

Blooms late winter and early spring.

Slightly acid, well-drained soil, in sun or light shade, moisture in fall and winter. Zone 8.

Plant in spring or late summer, setting the rootstocks just below the surface of the soil.

Use in the sunny border with other perennials, or in front of shrubs in the shrub border. Attractive ornamentals for warmer regions, especially those with wet winters and springs and dry summers.

Bulbinella cauda-felis. South Africa. Similar to *B. nutans* but shorter. Leaves present at flowering time but not always fully developed. Flowers in slender raceme, ⅓ in. (8 mm) across, white (pinkish in bud) or yellow, late spring to early summer.

Bulbinella nutans. South Africa. Leaves basal, linear, narrow, light green, with many veins. Flowers yellow to creamy white, very small but many in a spike, the lower ones withered before the entire spike has developed, resulting in a long flowering period of 3 to 10 weeks, beginning in late winter.

Caladium hybrids
Angel wings, elephant's-ear

Rhizome tuberous. Plant height 12–24 in. (30–60 cm). Leaves variously-shaped and colored; leaf stalks often variegated. The spadix is divided into three zones: the top is gray-yellow and bears male flowers; the center is whitish gray, with sterile flowers; and the lower portion produces light yellow female flowers. The spathe covering the flowers is hooded, and the lower portion is rolled.

Bloom insignificant.

Very rich soil with a liberal amount of peat moss, in bright light but not direct sunshine, ample moisture and high humidity. Protect from wind. Zones 10–12.

Potted caladiums with other shade-loving plants (International Flower Bulb Center)

Caladium 'Aaron' (International Flower Bulb Center)

Caladium 'Blaze' (International Flower Bulb Center)

Plant in spring, 2–3 in. (5–7.5 cm) deep, 1–2 in. (2.5–5 cm) apart if bulb is 1½ in. (4 cm) in diameter, 12 in. (30 cm) apart if bulb is 3 in. (7.5 cm) in diameter.

Use for their brightly colored leaves where summer temperatures and humidity are high. Can be grown in containers, provided there is no exposure to direct sunlight or wind. Good for summer display in greenhouses. They may be sold as container plants or dormant tubers.

'**Aaron**', white leaf and veins with wide, dark green border.

'**Blaze**', red leaf and veins with olive green border.

'**Candidum**', leaf almost entirely white with green border and dark green veins.

'**Florida Sunrise**', green leaf, white spots, and bright pink major veins.

'**Frieda Hemple**', bright red leaves with deeper red veins and green border, a sturdy plant that can stand a little wind.

'**Jody**', narrow, arrow-shaped leaves, red between white veins, green border.

'**Kathleen**', pink leaf and veins with green border.

Caladium 'Rosebud' (International Flower Bulb Center)

'**Rosebud**', leaves pink, white, and green.

'**Mrs. Arno Nehrling**', a selection of *Caladium bicolor*, fine, dark green leaf with network of lighter green veins and a crimson major vein.

CALOCHORTUS
Mariposa lily, fairy lantern

A genus of about 70 species from western North America. The bulbs are small and tunicated. The plants have swordlike, basal leaves; in species from warmer areas, the leaves are usually withered by flowering time in late spring to early summer. The flowers are held on thin but sturdy stems, branching in most species. The flower form is diverse: fairy lanterns, globe tulips, butterfly tulips, star tulip, cats' ears, and mariposa lilies. The inner three perianth segments (the petals) are broader and larger than the outer ones (the sepals). Most species have distinct hairs in zones on the upper surface of the petals; the microscopic characteristics of these hairs and the shape of the petal markings and nectary are important in identifying species. The sepals generally have less color than the petals and are greenish toward the base. There are six stamens.

Well-drained soil with a moderate amount of organic matter, in full sun, moisture in winter and early spring, dry in summer. Zones 8–9.

Plant in fall, 4–6 in. (10–15 cm) deep.

Use in warm, dry gardens where unusual and beautiful flowers are wanted. Not attractive in containers.

Calochortus barbatus. Mexico. Stems 1–3 ft. (30–90 cm). Leaves linear, pointed, 9–12 in. (22.5–30 cm). Bulbils produced in leaf axils. Flowers nodding, deep yellow, often with purplish markings on outer surface; petal margins fringed; interior covered with hairs; late summer.

Calochortus luteus. United States. Stems 12–18 in. (30–45 cm), with few branches. Lower leaves linear, 4–8 in. (10–20 cm) long; upper reduced. Flowers upward-facing, to five per plant, clear yellow with brown blotch at base of petal; hairs on lower part of petals; late spring to early summer. 'Golden Orb', great cut flowers.

Calochortus venustus. United States. Stems 8–24 in. (20–60 cm). Great color range: white, yellow, purple, orange, or red, with elaborate markings on petals. Flowers erect, more than 2 in. (5 cm) across, inner segments hairy, often with two zones of color; sepals darker.

Calochortus venustus (International Flower Bulb Center)

CAMASSIA
Camas, quamash

A genus of six species from the Americas closely allied to *Scilla*. They are very attractive plants. The leaves are long and linear, becoming lax as they age. The flowers are borne in long racemes with either upright or horizontal pedicels. In some species, the withered flowers persist on the developing seed capsule; along with the color of the flowers, this features is used in differentiating among species.

Any garden soil, in full sun (but can tolerate light shade during the hottest part of the day), moisture in spring and summer.

Camassia leichtlinii

Camassia quamash

Camassia quamash, detail

Plant in fall, 4–5 in. (10–12.5 cm) deep.

Use in masses in a variety of habitats, especially near streams and grassy swales where moisture is high during the growing season.

Camassia cusickii. United States. Bulb very large, heavy, to 5 in. (12.5 cm) long. Stems to 30 in. (75 cm) or more. Leaves to 2 in. (5 cm) wide, 20 in. (50 cm) long. Flowers numerous, usually pale blue; pedicels horizontal, turning up at ends; early summer. Withered tepals do not cover developing seed capsule. Zones 5–9. **'Zwanenburg'**, intense blue.

Camassia leichtlinii. United States, Canada. Bulb ½–1½ in. (12–40 mm) across. Stems to 3 ft. (90 cm) or more. Leaves to 1 in. (2.5 cm) wide, seldom more than 2 ft. (60 cm) long. Pedicels intermediate between horizontal and upright. Flower colors vary; tepals twist around developing capsule. One of best garden species. Zones 3–9. **'Alba'**, white. **Var.** *leichtlinii*, white. **'Plena'**, double creamy white to yellow. **'Semi-**

plena', greenish white, semidouble. **Var.** *suksdorfii*, deep purplish blue; its cultivars **'Blauwe Donau'** ("Blue Danube"), dark blue; **'Caerulea'**, vivid deep blue; and **'Electra'**, rich blue.

Camassia quamash. Canada, United States. Stems 1–2 ft. (30–60 cm). Flower color deep to pale blue and white. Withering tepals may drop away or cover capsule. Pedicels from horizontal to erect. Mid to late spring. Zones 5–9. **Subsp.** *azurea*, grayish leaves, light blue-violet flowers. **Subsp.** *breviflora*, gray-green leaves, blue to deep blue-violet flowers. **Subsp.** *intermedia*, green leaves, pale blue-violet flowers. **Subsp.** *linearis*, green leaves, deep blue-violet flowers. **Subsp.** *maxima*, grayish leaves, deep blue-violet flowers. **'Orion'**, deep blue flowers. **'San Juan'**, even deeper blue flowers. **Subsp.** *utahensis*, gray leaves, pale blue-violet flowers. **Subsp.** *walpolei*, green leaves, pale blue or blue-violet flowers.

CANNA
Canna lily

A genus of nine tropical species. Rootstock a fleshy rhizome with many rounded projections. Stem height varies: very dwarf (18–24 in., 45–60 cm), dwarf (25–30 in., 61–75 cm), standard (31–48 in., 76–120 cm), and very tall (more than 48 in., 120 cm). Leaves large-bladed, strongly veined. Flower and leaf colors vary, depending on cultivar. Flower consists of three mostly green sepals, three long petals, and up to five broad, colorful petaloid stamens. One stamen forms the lower "lip" of the flower. Fruit a three-celled capsule bearing many hard black seeds.

Blooms late summer.

Humus-rich soil, in full sun, high humidity, plenty of moisture, and a long warm season. Zones 8–12.

Plant in spring, 4–6 in. (10–15 cm) deep and 18–24 in. (45–60 cm) apart.

Use in a summer border for their bright flowers and handsome foliage. Remains attractive throughout the season. The smaller forms can be used in containers to highlight deck, patio, or entrance gardens. All types are very popular for summer bedding in public landscapes.

Canna 'Phasion' (Sally Ferguson)

Canna 'President' (International Flower Bulb Center)

Canna dwarf hybrids along a fence

Canna 'Richard Wallace' (International Flower Bulb Center)

'Black Knight', standard, bronze leaves, red flowers.

'Cherry Red', very dwarf, bright red with dark leaves.

'City of Portland', standard, green leaves, rose pink flowers.

'Pfitzer's Salmon Pink', dwarf, green leaves.

'Phasion' (Tropicanna™), very tall, orange flowers, dark leaves striped with red.

'President', standard, green leaves, bright red flowers.

'Roi Humbert' ("King Humbert"), very tall, at over 6 ft. (1.8 m), bronze leaves, red flowers.

'Richard Wallace', standard, green leaves, bright yellow flowers.

Seven Dwarfs Group, very short, yellow, salmon, pink, red, or crimson flowers.

Cardiocrinum giganteum

Himalaya. Stems tall and stout, often 4–6 in. (10–15 cm) across at base, 9 ft. (2.7 m) or more in height. Basal leaves form a rosette; others scattered up the stem. Leaves 18 in. (45 cm) long and almost as wide. Flowers 6–25 per stem, narrowly trumpet-shaped, to 6 in. (15 cm) across, very fragrant, slightly pendent; tepals tinted green when young, quickly turning pure white outside; interior pure white, flushed purplish toward base.

Cardiocrinum giganteum

Blooms in late summer.

Well-drained, humus-rich soil, in dappled shade, evenly moist. Protect leaves from damage by late frosts. Mulch to minimize damage from thawing and freezing. Zones 7–9.

Plant so top of bulb just breaks the soil surface.

Use as a stunning, tall accent against a solid background of evergreens, such as rhododendrons. It needs a spacious setting in light woodland to develop to its full potential.

Var. yunnanense, often 4–6 ft. (1.2–1.8 m) tall, stems dark brown, young foliage bronze-tinted, flowers often retain greenish tinge even when mature.

Chasmanthe floribunda

South Africa. Corm flattened. Stem branching, to 4 ft. (1.2 m). Leaves about 14 in. (35 cm) long, 2 in. (5 cm) wide, sword-shaped, tapering to a sharp point, arranged in a fan, coarse to the touch. The most floriferous species, often up to 30 flowers per stem, 12–15 per branch. Flowers abundant,

Chasmanthe floribunda

Chasmanthe floribunda var. *duckittii* (Jack Hobbs)

tubular, with the lower parts pinched and much shorter than the upper parts, flaring into separate lobes at the mouth of the tube, orange-red, tube often with yellow stripe; upper tepals form a hood over the lower ones. Upper buds often are still very small and carried closely together on the flattened flower spike while the lower flowers are fully open. The initial flowers are long past before the entire flower spike has fully developed, so the plants are in flower for a considerable time.

Blooms late spring.

Average soil, in full sun or light shade, moisture in winter and early spring. Zones 9–11.

Plant corms in fall or spring, 3 in. (7.5 cm) deep, 10 in. (25 cm) apart.

Use as a good, long-lasting cut flower. Should become more popular in the warmer and drier parts of the United States because plants are dormant in summer (and thus resistant to summer drought).

Var. *duckittii*, primrose yellow.

CHIONODOXA
Glory of the snow

A genus of about eight species from Crete, Cyprus, and Turkey. One of the finest early flowering bulbs. Closely related to *Scilla*, but the perianth segments are united at the base, forming a short tube, and the flattened filaments form a cone in the center of the flower. The plants grow from an egg-shaped bulb with a thin, fragile brown tunic. The leaves are basal, and not numerous; often only two are produced. The stems are short at flowering time and elongate as the seed ripens. The flowers are borne in loose racemes in late winter to early spring; depending on the species, the number per stem ranges from one to more than 10. The flowers are blue (though pinkish and white forms occur), with zones of white.

Blooms in early spring.

Well-drained soil, in sun, moisture in winter and spring. Zones 4–7.

Chiondoxa luciliae (International Flower Bulb Center)

Plant in fall, 3 in. (7.5 cm) deep.

Use in the rock garden or the front of the border for its very early flowers. Can also be planted in containers to be brought indoors.

Chiondoxa forbesii. Turkey. A variable species. Stems to 6 in. (15 cm). Flowers to 12 per stem, drooping slightly, deep blue with white center, as are the filaments. **'Alba'**, pure white. **'Naburn Blue'**, dark blue with white center. **'Siehei'**, exceptionally free-flowering. **'Tmoli'**, bright blue, 4 in. (10 cm) tall.

Chiondoxa luciliae. Turkey. Flowers many, small, in a one-sided raceme. **'Alba'**, large pure white. **'Gigantea'**, pale blue, flowers to 1 in. (2.5 cm) wide. **'Pink Giant'**, taller than type, dull pink. **'Rosea'**, pink. **'Zwanenburg'**, vigorous growing.

Chiondoxa sardensis. Turkey. Stems to 4 in. (10 cm). Flowers deep gentian blue with small white eye.

CLIVIA
Natal lily, thong lily

A genus of about four species of evergreen amaryllids from South Africa. Though often regarded as bulbs in the loose sense, they have rootstocks consisting mostly of the bases of the leaves, little if at all modified for storage. Their native habitats are shady areas, mostly where there is abundant winter moisture. Clivias form thick clumps where few other plants interfere with their spread. The flowers, borne in umbels, are quite striking—large and bright, in shades of red, orange, and yellow. They are broadly tubular or funnel-shaped. The dark green, strap-shaped leaves are broad and thick; the bases are sheathed.

Well-drained, humus-rich soil, in light or dappled shade, moisture always available. Zones 9–11.

Plant so the lighter-colored part of the lower leaves is in the soil, at least 12 in. (30 cm) apart.

Clivia miniata

Clivia nobilis

Clivia miniata var. citrina

Top-dress with good topsoil every other year and give weak feedings of organic fertilizer in late summer until the flower stems emerge.

Use in mild climates in the shady garden and under trees where they can be left undisturbed. Make superb container plants and can be brought indoors when in flower. Their tolerance of neglect makes them useful for indoor commercial plantings in offices or shopping malls.

Clivia miniata. Bush lily, flame lily, forest lily. Stems stout, to 2 ft. (60 cm) or more. Leaves deep green, 2–3 in. (5–7.5 cm) wide, strap-shaped. Flowers more trumpet-shaped than tubular, outward-facing rather than pendent, produced in winter and long-lasting. Inner segments broader than outer ones. Throat of flowers often lighter in color, sometimes yellow. Color varies, usually bright orange, sometimes redder. The usual flowering season is spring, but my plants in San Francisco often bloom from fall to spring. **'Aurea'** and **var.** *citrina* are yellow forms. **'Striata'**, variegated leaves.

Clivia nobilis. Red bush lily. Stems 24–30 in. (60–75 cm). Leaves fleshy, strap-shaped, dark green, to 3 ft. (90 cm) long, 10 in. (25 cm) wide. Flowers often 50 or more, cylindrical, pendent, and overlapping, so that inflorescence is umbrella-shaped. Tepals reddish orange, fading toward tips, with a green zone on the tips, darkest at the margin. Spring.

COLCHICUM
Autumn crocus, meadow saffron

A genus of 45 very poisonous species in the eastern Mediterranean, extending east into Iran and Turkestan and west into Europe, including Great Britain. Amateur gardeners may confuse *Crocus* and *Colchicum*, largely as a result of the latter's common names. Flower color helps distinguish them: colchicum flowers are pinkish or rose lavender (though white forms exist), whereas fall-blooming crocuses are blue-lavender or white. Corms can be to 4 in. (10 cm) across, and very heavy. The tunic is brown and leathery when mature and extends above the body of the corm to ground level; this "neck" provides a pathway for the emerging flowers. The length

Colchicum speciosum (Jack Hobbs)

of the leaves varies according to species but can reach 12 in. (30 cm) long and half as wide. The leaves can thus smother low plants growing nearby. The leaves wither by mid summer. The seed capsule ripens in early summer. The flowers vary greatly in size depending on the species, but those grown in gardens are large-flowered—as much as 6 in. (15 cm) from soil surface to the tip of the flower.

Deep, well-drained, moisture-retentive soil with a moderate amount of organic matter, in full sun (in hot, dry areas give shade for the hottest part of the day), moisture until leaves start to die back, then withhold water.

Plant in late summer, setting the neck even with the soil surface or the "shoulder" (the broadest part of the corm) 2–3 in. (5–7.5 cm) below the surface.

Use to bring color at an unusual time of year. Not good as container plants. The smallest species are suitable for the warm rock garden.

Colchicum speciosum 'Album' (Jack Hobbs)

Colchicum autumnale

Colchicum 'Autumn Queen', lilac with white throat, silvery white tessellation.

Colchicum autumnale. Meadow saffron, naked boys. Europe. Corm large, elliptical. Leaves five to eight, produced in spring, about 10 in. (25 cm) long and 1 in. (2.5 cm) wide. Flowers pale pink and leafless, numerous, up to six per corm, reaching 4–6 in. (10–15 cm) and soon flopping over; late summer to early fall. Zones 5–9. **'Alboplenum'**, robust double white. **'Album'**, weak-growing albino. **'Nancy Lindsay'**, large flowers with deep violet tube. **'Pleniflorum'**, double lilac pink.

Colchicum byzantinum. Origin uncertain. Corm 3 in. (7.5 cm) across, short and broad, with red-brown tunic. Leaves emerge in spring. Flowers very numerous, tube 3 in. (7.5 cm) and white, tepals oval and 2 in. (5 cm), pale lilac pink with white midline above, corresponding to distinct keel below. White styles exceed pale brown stamens; pollen deep yellow. Stigma distinctly hooked, crimson-purple. Early fall. Zones 6–9. **'Album'**, often flushed pink at tips, possibly deeper when exposed to colder temperatures. It is quite amazing that even after 400 years, this species has retained its vigor; many modern descendants of bulbous plants do not exhibit such stamina.

Colchicum cilicicum. Turkey. Similar to C. byzantinum but flowers a little later, and leaves emerge soon after the lilac-pink, moderate-sized flowers. Zones 6–9. **'Purpureum'**, deeper rose lavender.

Colchicum corsicum. Corsica. Flowers small, rosy lilac; late summer. Zone 9.

Colchicum 'Dick Trotter', large upright deep pink, tessellated.

Colchicum 'Disraeli', magenta with pale center, large.

Colchicum 'Lilac Wonder', narrow, amethyst-violet tepals with white midlines.

Colchicum speciosum. Turkey. Corm to 4 in. (10 cm) long, proportionately slender. Leaves to 12 in. (30 cm) long or more, 3 in. (7.5 cm) wide, bright green, glossy. Flowers to 12 in. (30 cm) tall with tube, slender goblet-shaped; pale to deep reddish violet, with paler to white throat. Zones 6–9. **'Album'**, strong-growing, pure white with a

Colchicum 'The Giant' (International Flower Bulb Center)

soft green tube. '**Atrorubens**', dark purple. One of the finest species for the garden. One bulb covers 1 sq. ft. (930 sq. cm) in two seasons if left undisturbed.

Colchicum '**The Giant**', 10–12 in. (25–30 cm) tall, very free-flowering violet with large white throat zone.

Colchicum '**Violet Queen**', flowers faintly checkered with imperial purple and white lines in throat; distinctive orange anthers.

Colchicum '**Waterlily**', large double, often with 20 tepals, lilac rose, but flowers often fall over and stock may be weakening.

Convallaria majalis
Lily-of-the-Valley

Northern Europe temperate zone. Rootstock a horizontal rhizome, producing pips from which the flowering stems and foliage arise. Leaves two or three, heart-shaped, 8 in. (20 cm) long, clasping the flowering stem at the base, then widening to wrap around the fragrant flower spike. Flowering stem 6–10 in. (15–25 cm) high, carrying 5–15 small, pendent, tubby bell-shaped white flowers in a one-sided raceme.

Blooms in late spring.

Humus-rich soil, in shade, moisture from early spring through mid summer. Never allow to become completely dry. Zones 3–9.

Plant in fall or late winter, 2–3 in. (5–7.5 cm) deep, 6 in. (15 cm) apart,

Use as a groundcover in shady, moist spots, especially north-facing borders. It spreads rapidly and may overrun other plants. The foliage withers after mid summer, leaving a bare spot until the following spring. A superb cut flower, much in demand by florists for its sentimental associations and exquisite fragrance.

'**Aureovariegata**', leaves striped gold, with an unfortunate propensity to revert to plain green.

'**Flore Pleno**', double form, both white and pink forms are often offered.

'**Fortin's Giant**', robust, tall-growing, with larger leaves and a strong fragrance.

'**Hardwick Hall**', bluish leaves with thin yellow margins.

Convallaria majalis (International Flower Bulb Center)

Convallaria majalis 'Fortin's Giant' (Klehm's Song Sparrow Perennial Farm)

Convallaria majalis 'Flore Pleno' (Klehm's Song Sparrow Perennial Farm)

Convallaria majalis var. *rosea* (Klehm's Song Sparrow Perennial Farm)

Corydalis solida (David M. Ward)

'Prolificans', a curious if not beautiful form in which individual florets are replaced by a little cluster of smaller, single flowers.

Var. *rosea*, medium pink flowers, smaller than the usual white ones.

Corydalis solida

Temperate regions throughout the Northern Hemisphere. An extremely variable species. Tuber oblong to globe-shaped. Leaves two to three on long stalks, divided into two, leaflets deeply but evenly divided. Stems to 10 in. (25 cm). Flowers purple, nodding, to 20 per stem, lower petals with a prominent pouch at base. Corolla usually pale lavender-pink. Outer petals have broad wings; inner petals pale, marked on inner surface with dark reddish purple at the tip. Spur straight.

Blooms in spring.

Well-drained soil, in part shade. Zones 5–9.

Plant in the fall, 2–3 in. (5–7.5 cm) deep.

Use in woodland and rock gardens.

Subsp. *incisa*, bracts with lobes that are again divided or toothed.

Subsp. *solida* 'Beth Evans', soft pink with a white flush on the spur.

Subsp. *solida* 'George Baker', brilliant orange-red.

Subsp. *solida* 'Nettleton Pink', vigorous, rich pink.

CRINUM
Milk lily, Orinoco lily

A genus of 100 or more evergreen and deciduous species from tropical and subtropical regions. All have very large, rounded bulbs with long necks. The entire bulb may exceed 12 in. (30 cm) across. The leaves are usually arranged in one plane in two opposite ranks, and are broad and numerous, often 20 or more. The flowers also are large, borne in umbels on stout stems from 2 to 4 ft. (60–120 cm) tall. There are many flowers in the umbel but seldom more than five to seven open

Crinum americanum

at one time. Individual flowers may exceed 8 in. (20 cm) across. The pedicels are either absent or short, often curved so that the flowers face somewhat down. The base of the flower is a long, narrow tube, and the tepals flare more or less widely toward the mouth. The tepals are thick, and the outer ones usually have a red to crimson midrib.

Blooms late summer, but species from the tropics may flower year-round.

Humus-rich soil, in full sun, plenty of moisture. Feed with liquid organic fertilizer during summer until plants send up their flowering stems. Give overhead protection during cold spells in areas where frosts are likely but not severe.

Plant in early summer, making sure the rounded part of the bulb is buried but that the neck is aboveground

Use as greenhouse subjects in areas where frosts are common, or as container plants brought indoors during winter. In milder climates, they look well where the flowers can be seen against a background of summer-flowering bulbs. In the herbaceous border, they should be considered only as highlights. Good in large containers, where they can be left undisturbed for a number of years.

Crinum americanum. Florida swamp lily, swamp lily. United States, Jamaica. Bulb globe-shaped, 3–4 in. (7.5–10 cm) across. Stems 18–36 in. (45–90 cm). Flowers white tinged green or purple-crimson, crimson on reverse, produced sporadically from spring to fall. Zones 9–11.

Crinum 'Ellen Bosanquet'. An old but still popular hybrid with fragrant reddish flowers.

Crinum macowanii. Cape coast lily, pajama lily. Zimbabwe, South Africa. Stems to 4 ft. (1.2 m). Leaves deciduous, to 3 ft. (90 cm) long and 3–4 in. (7.5–10 cm) wide. Flowers large, trumpet-shaped, white to pale pink with crimson central stripe; anthers black, a distinctive trait; late summer. Fruit round and knobby, containing large, irregular seeds. Deserves greater recognition in warm climates. Zone 9.

Crinum moorei. Cape coast lily. South Africa. Stems to 4 ft. (1.2 m). Leaves to 3 ft. (90 cm)

Crinum 'Ellen Bosanquet' (Jack Hobbs)

Crinum ×powellii (International Flower Bulb Center)

Crinum macowanii

Crinum ×powellii, detail (International Flower Bulb Center)

long, 4 in. (10 cm) wide. Flowers white or pale pink, spring to summer. Unlike many other species, needs some shade in hot areas. Requires much moisture in summer but drier winter conditions. A favorite for the cool greenhouse. Zones 8–11.

Crinum ×powellii. Garden hybrid (*C. bulbispermum* × *C. moorei*). Stems 24–30 in. (60–75 cm). Leaves to 4 ft. (1.2 m) long, 4 in. (10 cm) wide, narrowing toward tip. Flowers pure white to midpink, to 4 in. (10 cm) across, fragrant, to 15 per stem, late summer. Zones 7–10. One of the best for garden use and should be the first *Crinum* to try in the garden. '**Album**', pure white. '**Harlemense**', pale shell-pink. '**Krelagei**', deep pink, large flowers.

Crocosmia (Jack Hobbs)

CROCOSMIA
Montbretia

The flowers have six perianth segments which flare widely. The six stamens are often longer than the perianth segments. The sword-shaped leaves are arranged in a flat fan and have a matte surface. The flower stem rises from the rootstock among the leaves and has several shorter leaves on its lower part. Flower colors are yellow, gold, orange, and red.

Light, sandy, humus-rich, well-drained soil, in sun or light shade, ample moisture in spring and early summer, drier in late summer.

Plant in late winter, spring, or fall, 3–4 in. (7.5–10 cm) deep, 8–12 in. (20–30 cm) apart.

Use in narrow borders, for example, beside a driveway or path. They look best planted in bold groups. Once established, they demand little care and crowd out other plants. They are good in containers, especially for late-summer flowering, and they provide good cut flowers. Where well adapted, they are useful for public and commercial landscape planting. Especially suitable near the seacoast.

Crocosmia ×*crocosmiiflora*. Garden hybrid (*C. aurea* × *C. pottsii*). Stems to 3 ft. (90 cm) but usually less. Leaves sword-shaped, coarse but not unattractive. Flowers in a zigzag, upright, loose stalk; perianth funnel-shaped; slender tube about 1 in. (2.5 cm) long. Flowers mostly orange-scarlet, other colors in cultivars. Long flowering period, late summer into fall. Zones 5–9. 'Carmin Brillant', stems 2 ft. (60 cm), flowers orange-red. 'Citronella', pleasant light lemon yellow, not very free-flowering. 'Emily McKenzie', stems 2 ft. (60 cm), flowers orange. 'His Majesty', flowers large, deep orange-scarlet, crimson on reverse. 'Jackanapes', stems 2 ft. (60 cm), flowers red and yellow. 'James Coey', stems 2 ft. (60 cm), flowers red. 'Lady Hamilton', stems 3 ft. (90 cm), flowers orange-yellow. 'Queen of Spain', stems 3 ft. (90 cm), flowers orange-red,

Crocosmia 'Lucifer'

Crocosmia masoniorum (International Flower Bulb Center)

summer. **'Solfatare'**, stems 2 ft. (60 cm), leaves bronze, flowers clear yellow, summer. **'Star of the East'**, flowers pale orange-yellow, showing up well in shade. **'Vesuvius'**, stems 2 ft. (60 cm), flowers red, fall.

Crocosmia **'Lucifer'**. Stems to 48 ft. (1.2 m). Flowers true red. The hardiest hybrid.

Crocosmia masoniorum. South Africa. Stems to 2 ft. (60 cm) long, arching to nearly horizontal. Leaves pleated, held in a fan, 18–24 in. (45–60 cm). Flowers brilliant orange-red. Zones 7–9.

CROCUS

A genus of more than 80 species distributed over much of Europe, especially around the Mediterranean, in North Africa, and in Asia as far east as Afghanistan. Although they are a symbol of early spring, many species in fact flower in autumn. Some corms have ring-shaped tunics; others have fibers that run parallel from top to bottom; still others have shell-like tunics with overlapping scales. Other characteristics that aid in the identification of species are whether the leaves emerge before or after the flowers, the number of leaves, and their growth habit. The most obvious traits are the color and marking of the tepals and the color of the anthers. Crocus flowers range from blue-lavender to purple, pure white, and cream through yellow to orange. Many species have a lighter throat, and a few have a darker zone in the throat. The three outer tepals are often a different shade from the inner three on the reverse (the outside, when the flower is closed), and in many species they are veined, striped, or feathered with deep purple outside.

Blooms spring or fall, depending on the species.

Average garden soil, well drained to at least 6 in. (15 cm) deep, in part shade with at least four hours of sun per day. Fertilize in fall and spring. Hardiness variable.

Plant autumn-flowering species in late summer, spring-flowering species in fall, 3–4 in. (7.5–10 cm) deep, 6 in. (15 cm) apart.

Use in masses for early spring and fall color. Naturalized in lawns or among other early flowers, they prolong the season of color in herbaceous and shrub borders. Many do well planted under fine-textured groundcovers, such as thyme. All kinds grow well in containers, which can be brought into the house. If they are removed to a colder area at night, the flowering period will be prolonged. It is possible to have crocuses in flower from fall to spring.

Crocus biflorus. Scotch crocus. Italy, Sicily, Rhodes Island, Turkey; naturalized in Europe. Corm tunic ring-shaped. Flowers white or lilac blue, with three purple or brownish-purple bands on outer segments, sometimes fine purple feathering, or unmarked with silvery or pale buff exterior, fragrant, early spring. Zone 4. **Subsp.** *adamii*, lilac or white flowers, strongly striped deep purple on exterior. **Subsp.** *alexandri*, white flowers with broad, deep purple central zone on outer segments, a white throat, and wide leaves that are not well-developed at flowering. **Subsp.** *crewei*, gray-green leaves, blackish-maroon anthers. **Subsp.** *isauricus*, lilac or white flowers, striped or speckled on exterior with purple or gray-purple. **Subsp.** *melantherus*, white flowers striped or

Crocus spp., planted in grass (International Flower Bulb Center)

speckled purple or gray on exterior, blackish anthers; fall. **Subsp.** *tauri*, pale to midlilac flowers, without dark stripes but sometimes finely veined or feathered; throat pale yellow. **Subsp.** *weldenii*, white flowers without stripes, a white throat; its cultivar **'Fairy'**, many white flowers flushed gray-blue on outer segments.

Crocus cancellatus. Turkey, Syria, Lebanon, Israel. Corm tunic coarsely netted. Leaves gray-green, appear after flowers. Flowers to 2 in. (5 cm), pale to midlilac-blue; throat pale yellow; outer segments feathered with violet at base; style many-branched, orange; anthers yellow; early to late fall. Zone 5. **Subsp.** *mazziaricus*, white or mid to deep lilac flowers, style much longer than anthers; may have a deep purple zone at throat. **Subsp.** *pamphylicus*, white anthers.

Crocus cartwrightianus. Wild saffron. Greece. Flowers pale to deep lilac purple or white, strongly veined darker; throat white or lilac; anthers yellow; mid to late fall. Zone 8.

Crocus chrysanthus. Balkan Peninsula, Greece, Turkey. Corm tunic membranous to shell-like, ring-shaped at base. Leaves present at flowering. Flowers fragrant, bright yellow to orange; outer segments feathered, striped, or flushed bronze or purple; anthers yellow; late winter. Zones 6–8. **'Advance'**, pale yellow and lavender bicolor. **'Blue Pearl'**, large soft blue with bronze base and golden throat, darker violet-blue exterior. **'Cream Beauty'**, large vigorous cream-yellow. **'Goldilocks'**, deep yellow with purple base. **'Ladykiller'**, white with rich purple exterior segments. **'Mariette'**, large, soft yellow inside, purplish outside. **'Skyline'**, pale blue-lilac with violet blotch and veining on exterior. **'Zwanenburg Bronze'**, large deep gold, flushed red-brown outside.

Crocus etruscus. Italy. Corm tunic coarsely netted. Leaves present at flowering. Flowers large, to 5 in. (12.5 cm), bright lilac blue, variably striped with deeper lilac on exterior; throat yellow; style three-branched, orange; early to mid spring. Zones 6–8. **'Zwanenburg'**, vigorous growing.

Crocus goulimyi. Greece. Corm tunic hard and shell-like, splitting lengthwise at base. Leaves appear with flowers. Flowers soft blue-lilac, broadly bowl-shaped, to 4 in. (10 cm) tall, mid to late fall. Produces many offsets. Very beautiful. Zones 7–8.

Crocus kotschyanus. Turkey, Russia. Corm smooth, irregular, and flattened. Leaves appear after flowers, persisting through winter. Flowers to 3 in. (7.5 cm), pale lilac with darker veins, throat whitish with yellow blotches, early fall. Zones 6–7. **Var.** *leucopharynx*, vigorous growing, a white throat without yellow blotches at base.

Crocus laevigatus. Greece. Corm completely covered by hard, smooth, dark brown tunic. Leaves appear before flowers. Flowers to 3 in. (7.5 cm), lavender-blue, outer tepals feathered deep lilac mauve; throat pale yellow; style deep orange, many-branched and featherlike; anthers creamy white; late fall to mid winter. Zone 7. **'Fontenayi'**, not distinct from the type but reliably free-flowering and increases fast.

Crocus sativus. Saffron. Origin uncertain. Corm large, tunic silky with densely netted fibers. Leaves appear just before flowers and may reach 12 in. (30 cm). Flowers lilac purple with deeper throat, early to mid autumn. Style branches very long, often protruding beyond the closed flower and flopping to the side; these are harvested and dried as saffron. Requires deep planting in rich, warm soil and frequent division to flower well. Zones 6–8.

Crocus sieberi. Crete. Corm tunic fibrous, finely netted. Leaves present at flowering, in mid spring. Flowers to 3 in. (7.5 cm), fragrant, white interior; throat yellow to orange, hairless. Zones 6–8. **Subsp.** *atticus*, corm with a persistent fibrous neck, flowers pale to deep lilac blue within. **'Hubert Edelsten'**, lilac, strikingly banded and tipped deep purple and white. **Subsp.** *sublimis*, corm tunic finely netted, throat hairy, flowers lilac-blue, often with darker tips, sometimes a white zone between the main segment color and yellow throat. **Subsp.** *sublimis* **'Tricolor'**, startlingly colored with a deep yellow throat, a band of bright white, and rich lilac-blue perianth blade. **'Violet Queen'**, small midviolet flowers.

Crocus speciosus. Crimea, Caucasus, Turkey, Iran. Corms large, ring-shaped at the base, producing many cormlets. Leaves relatively wide, appearing long after flowers and attaining 8 in. (20 cm) or more. Flowers to 6 in. (15 cm) on long tubes, narrowly goblet-shaped, pale to deep violet-blue with purple veins; throat white to pale yellow; anthers yellow; style yellow to deep orange, with many slender branches; mid autumn. Zones 6–8. 'Aitchisonii', pale lavender-violet, large. 'Albus', vigorous, pure white. 'Artabir', near-blue, inner segments lighter, tube flushed blue. 'Cassiope', very tall aster-blue with yellowish base. 'Conqueror', strong blue-lavender. One of the showiest and hardiest fall-flowering species for gardens, tolerant of summer water and increasing well by offsets and self-sowing.

Crocus tommasinianus. Yugoslavia, Hungary, Bulgaria. Corm nearly spherical, with finely netted tunic. Leaves lax, well-developed at flowering in early spring. Flowers to 4 in. (10 cm), pale to deep lavender, often silvery on exterior, usually unmarked; throat white; style orange, divided into three branches much expanded and

fringed at tips. Zones 6–8. **Var.** *albus*, white. 'Barr's Purple', large rich purple-lilac. **Var.** *pictus*, tips of segments deep purple. **Var.** *roseus*, nearest to true pink in the genus. 'Ruby Giant', deep violet-purple, free-flowering. 'Whitewell Purple', reddish purple.

Crocus vernus. Europe, Ukraine. Corm tunic fibrous, slightly netted. Leaves present at flowering, sometimes short, sometimes well-developed. Flowers 3–5 in. (7.5–12.5 cm), mostly purple or lilac; tube purple; style usually deep yellow or orange, divided into three branches very frilled at the tips; exceeding or equal to anthers. Zones 6–8. **Subsp.** *albiflorus*, smaller flowers, usually white, style much shorter than anthers; well adapted to temperate gardens and the source of most of the larger-flowered Dutch crocuses. 'Flower Record', purple, good for forcing. 'Haarlem Gem', small, purple flowers with lighter outer segments. 'Jeanne d'Arc', white. 'Pickwick', white with purple stripes. 'Purpureus Grandiflorus', very large, purple. 'Queen of the Blues', lavender blue. 'Remembrance', silvery lavender. 'Snowstorm',

Crocus tommasinianus

Crocus 'Yellow Mammoth'

white. **'Striped Beauty'**, silvery with purple stripes.

Crocus **'Yellow Mammoth'**. Flowers large, yellow.

CYCLAMEN
Persian violet, alpine violet

A genus of about 20 species, most of which are from the Mediterranean region. Some species can be grown outdoors in fairly cold climates. The rootstock is a tuber. It does not produce offsets and increases in size throughout its lifetime; an old tuber of some species may be more than 1 ft. (30 cm) across, producing hundreds of flowers. The fibrous roots may emerge from the bottom, sides, or near the top of the tuber, depending on the species. The leaf and flower stalks arise directly from the tuber. The leaves are mostly heart- or arrow-shaped, and in many species are beautifully marked with deeper green, gray, or silvery spots or zones. The flowers are solitary, with five petals, always reflexed, sometimes curled, joined near the base in a short tube. The capsule is often drawn down to the soil level as it ripens by the spiraling of the stalk.

Crocus vernus

Cyclamen hederifolium
(Jack Hobbs)

Cyclamen persicum selections
from Goldsmith Seeds
(left to right): 'Sierra',
'Miracle', and 'Laser'

Cyclamen pseudibericum
(left) with a white-flowered
rhododendron (foreground)
and other potted plants

Blooms various times, depending on the species. It is possible to have species in flower throughout the year.

Loose, free-draining soil with a high percentage of leafmold, in shade, moisture in autumn, winter, and early spring, drier in summer. Hardiness varies by species.

Plant ½ in. (12 mm) deep.

Use florist cyclamens as house plants. Use the natural species in the woodland, rock garden, and shady corners where a low-growing plant with decorative leaves is wanted. They should remain undisturbed and allowed to increase by self-sowing; in favorable climates, this can eventually produce lovely drifts. They are easily grown in small containers to be brought indoors for color. In colder areas, many species perform well in frames protected from severe frost and snow.

Cyclamen coum. Bulgaria, Turkey, Caucasus, Lebanon, Israel. A widespread and extremely variable species. Roots produced from base of thick tuber. Leaves usually rounded, dark green with dull crimson underside, plain or with silvery markings (usually slight) on upper surface. Flowers short and broad, pink to crimson with deeper-colored zone at base; anthers yellow; on stems 4–5 in. (10–12.5 cm) tall; winter. Both leaf and flower stems creep for a short distance underground before emerging. Excellent garden plants which spread extensively in favorable climates. Zones 6–10. **Subsp.** *caucasicum*, pink, dark pink or white "eye" at base of petals, heart-shaped leaves with silver-gray marbling and toothed margin.

Cyclamen hederifolium. Sowbread. Southern Europe. Roots produced from upper surface of tuber; lower surface free of roots and somewhat rounded. Leaves show great variation in shape (round, ivy- or lance-shaped), in margins (smooth to crinkled), and in marking patterns; foliage persists from early fall to early summer. Flowers white to carmine, on stems 3–6 in. (7.5–15 cm) long; earlike lobes around mouth; late summer to early fall. Spreads rapidly by self-sowing where adapted. One of the finest species and the first choice for most gardens. Zones 6–9. **Var.** *confusum*, bright green, thick and fleshy leaves, margins lobed. **Var.** *hederifolium*, dark or gray-green leaves with prominent markings and finely toothed margin. **Var.** *hederifolium* **f.** *albiflorum* 'Album', flowers white with a red or purple blotch.

Cyclamen persicum. Mediterranean region. Rounded tubers root from base. Leaves vary in size and color, generally dark green zoned with lighter green markings, almost always heart-shaped. Flowers on tall stems, 6 in. (15 cm) or more, often fragrant, from white to deep purple-rose, winter to early spring. Parent of the popular florist cyclamen.

Cyclamen pseudibericum. Turkey. Tubers root from base. Leaves have serrated edge, and often yellowish-green mottling on surface; crimson undersurface. Flowers large, to 1 in. (2.5 cm) across, fragrant, deep purplish carmine with more intense color at base; early spring. Zone 11.

CYRTANTHUS
Fire lily

A genus of about 50 deciduous and evergreen species from South and East Africa. The bulbs are tunicated; those of some species grow partially exposed. All stems are hollow. The leaves are narrow, sometimes grasslike, and sometimes persistent—evergreen, in some species. They appear either with the flowers or after flowering, depending on the species. The flowers are borne in an umbel. They are tubular, usually flaring just a little at the mouth, but some species have spreading tepals. The tube is as much as 10 times longer than the lobes in some species. Certain species are fragrant, and flower colors range from red through pink to white or yellow. The fruit is an oblong capsule with many flattened black seeds.

Blooms late summer and fall, or in spring.

Well-drained, humus-rich soil, in full sun, adequate moisture when growing. Plants respond well to an organic liquid fertilizer while in growth. Zones 10–11.

Plant summer- or fall-flowering species in spring, spring-flowering species in fall, 2–3 in. (5–7.5 cm) deep, 5–6 in. (12.5–15 cm) apart.

Use as container plants.

Cyrtanthus contractus (syn. *Vallota contractus*). South Africa, Swaziland, Lesotho. Stems to 12 in. (30 cm). Leaves grasslike, often more than 12 in. (30 cm) long, appearing soon after flowers. Flowers scarlet, half nodding, to 2 in. (5 cm); usually late spring and summer, but may flower at any time of year.

Cyrtanthus mackenii (syn. *Vallota mackenii*). Ifafa lily. South Africa. Stems to 12 in. (30 cm). Leaves 8–12 in. (20–30 cm) long, evergreen, produced with flowers. Flowers fragrant, white, a little over 1 in. (2.5 cm) long, narrowly tubular, four or more per stem; not as pendent as many other species but seldom erect—usually horizontal or slightly erect; late summer. **Var. *cooperi***, yellow or cream, early to late spring.

Cyrtanthus speciosus (syn. *Vallota speciosa*). South Africa. Stems 6–7 in. (15–17.5 cm). Leaves deciduous. Flowers creamy white, striped red or pink, green and pink at base.

Cyrtanthus contractus (Jack Hobbs)

Cyrtanthus speciosus (Alpine Garden Society, United Kingdom)

DAHLIA

A genus of about 30 species in Mexico, Central America, and Colombia. The fleshy roots are tuberous. The stems branch at the base and again above. They are produced only from the lower part of the flowering stem. The flowers are carried on long stalks. Although most species in the wild produce only single flowers, some often have semidouble flowers. The singles have a yellow disk of female florets in the center, surrounded by a ring of male ray florets, in which the pistils are petal-like. A protective sheath envelops the developing ovary. In doubles, the number of male petal-like florets is greatly increased. Only rarely are disk florets entirely absent, and most flowers—even double ones—can produce at least some seeds. Dahlias are not necessarily self-sterile, but the male pollen of a flower ripens before the same flower's stigmata become receptive, so flowers are seldom self-pollinated.

Deep, humus-rich soil, in full sun, regular moisture in summer. Give weak but regular feedings of 15–15 15 fertilizer through mid summer, then 5–10–15 when buds appear. Pinch out the

Dahlia 'Kiwi Gloria', Cactus-flowered Group (Jack Hobbs)

Dahlia imperialis (Jack Hobbs)

Dahlia 'Sunshine', Single-flowered Group (Jack Hobbs)

bud at the tip of the stem when the plants are 4–6 in. (10–15 cm) tall to encourage bushier plants. After frost kills the top growth, cut off the stalks 4 or 5 in. (10–12.5 cm) above the ground. Zones 9–11.

Plant in late winter and early spring, two weeks before the last expected frost, 3–4 in. (7.5–10 cm) deep, 12–18 in. (30–45 cm) apart if low-growing, 3 ft. (90 cm) apart if expected to reach 3 ft. tall.

Use for late summer flowers. Make great cut flowers.

Dahlia imperialis. Tree dahlia. Mexico, Guatemala, San Salvador, Colombia, Costa Rica. Stems 6–30 ft. (1.8–9 m), usually branched only at base, swollen where the leaves are attached. Leaves have or three leaflets and are 3 ft. (90 cm) long. Flowers 6 in. (15 cm) across, white or pink with red markings at base, late summer.

Dahlia hybrids are divided into groups according to their flower shapes, three of which are illustrated here. **Single-flowered Group:** flowers open-centered, with one or two complete outer rows of florets surrounding a disc, usually about 4 in. (10 cm) across; ideal for summer bedding, being about 12 in. (30 cm) tall. **Decorative Group:** no visible central disc; flower fully double, with ray flower broad and flat or slightly rolled inward, often slightly twisted; heights of 3 to 10 ft. (90–300 cm), and flowers usually very large. **Cactus-flowered Group:** flowers double, no visible disc, ray florets long and pointed; margins petals strongly rolled inward for over half their length, ends cut or fringed.

Dicentra spectabilis
Bleeding heart

Siberia and Japan. Rootstock a rhizome with fleshy tubers. Stems 18–30 in. (45–75 cm). Leaves much cut, segments elliptical and wedge-shaped. Flowers pink to rosy crimson, in a graceful arching raceme; individual flowers 1 in. (2.5 cm) long. The two outer petals are reflexed or spreading, like little spurs, while the inner two petals are larger and held together over the style and anthers.

Dicentra spectabilis

Blooms late spring to early summer.

Deep, humus-rich soil, in shade. Liquid organic fertilizer can be applied as soon as growth is noticed in the spring. Care should be taken not to overfeed, or the plants become rank. Zones 6–9.

Plant 2–3 in. (5–7.5 cm) deep.

Use for the cool, partly shaded border and woodland garden:

'Alba', pure white.

'Pantaloons', pure white.

DICHELOSTEMMA

A genus of five species from western North America, where they grow in summer-dry grasslands. This genus is distinguished from *Triteleia* by the presence of three fertile stamens rather than six. The rootstock is a spherical corm. The linear leaves are V-shaped in cross section, all basal, and may be withered by flowering time.

Well-drained soil, in full sun, moderate moisture in fall and spring.

Plant 4–5 in. (10–12.5 cm) deep, 6 in. (15 cm) apart.

Dichelostemma congestum (International Flower Bulb Center)

Use for the showy, unusual flowers. Like other California grassland bulbs, these are suited to borders and naturalistic settings where dry conditions prevail in summer. Plants in groups of five to seven corms.

Dichelostemma congestum. United States, Canada. Stems to 3 ft. (90 cm). Leaves about ½ in. (12 mm) wide, to 18 in. (45 cm) long. Flowers to ¾ in. (2 cm) long, blue-violet; tubes very short; three fertile stamens, and three outer sterile stamens reduced to tiny stubs; late spring to early summer. Zone 8.

Dichelostemma ida-maia. California firecracker, firecracker flower. United States. Stems 20–36 in. (50–90 cm), often bent or slightly twisted. Leaves stiff, to 1½ in. (4 cm) wide and 20 in. (50 cm) long. Flowers numerous in dense umbels, about 1 in. (2.5 cm) long; tube bright red, long with very short reflexed lobes green to cream; early summer. The showy flowers make this the most desirable species for the garden. Zone 7.

DIERAMA
Flowering grass, angel's fishing rod

A genus of 44 species from Africa. Rootstock an annually renewed corm with a fibrous tunic. Stems to 6 ft. (1.8 m). Leaves stiff, to 3 ft. (90 cm) long, narrow, grasslike. The arching flower stem rises above the foliage, bending with the weight of the pendent flowers. The slender flower stalks move constantly in even the slightest breeze. The flowers open successively, so that the inflorescence persists over a long period.

Blooms late spring to early summer.

Well-drained, good soil, in full sun (although they appreciate afternoon shade in hot climates), ample moisture in spring and early summer. Feed in spring as new growth is made. Plants take at least a season to settle in and resent being transplanted. Zones 7–10.

Plant in late summer or early fall, 3–5 in. (7.5–12.5 cm) deep, 12–18 in. (30–45 cm) apart.

Use in the herbaceous perennial border in groups of five to seven or as isolated specimens by

Dierama pulcherrimum (Jack Hobbs)

Dierama pendulum

a water feature, just above the waterline where the soil is not constantly wet, so that the graceful stems and flowers are reflected in the water.

Dierama pendulum. Flowering grass. South Africa. Flowers to 1 in. (2.5 cm) long, whitish or varying from pink to purple, with widely spreading perianth.

Dierama pulcherrimum. Magenta wallflower. South Africa. Corms whitish, maturing with a thick tunic of dry, parallel fibers. Stems to 6 ft. (180 cm). Flowers large, bright purple to rich carmine; distinctive bracts, white with some browning at base, show well against colorful perianth segments. Tepals never spread widely from their conical base (as they do in *D. pendulum*).

DIETES
Wild iris

A genus of about six evergreen species from South Africa, Lord Howe Island, and Australia. The rootstock is a rhizome. The leaves are sword-shaped, relatively broad and tapering to a fine point, often quite long and leathery. The numerous flowers are iris-like in appearance but, in most species, last for only a day. The three outer perianth segments are broad; the three inner are narrower but often as long as the outer ones. The style is three-branched and petal-like, giving a full look to the flower. The nectar guide is quite prominent.

Any soil, in full sun, moisture in winter and spring, dry in summer. Zones 9–11.

Plant in late summer, just below the soil surface, 4–6 in. (10–15 cm) apart if short-growing, 18 in. (45 cm) apart if taller growing.

Use where a sturdy plant requiring little care is needed. They flower profusely over a long period.

Dietes bicolor. Peacock flower. South Africa. Stems to 2 ft. (60 cm) or more, much branched. Leaves to 30 in. (75 cm) long, 2 in. (5 cm) wide. Flowers numerous, light cream with brown blotches at the base of the broader segments; early spring, but some flowers are produced throughout summer.

Dietes grandiflora. East Africa, South Africa. Stems to 4 ft. (1.2 m). Leaves to 3 ft. (90 cm)

long, 4 in. (10 cm) wide. Flowers, perhaps the loveliest of the genus, pure white with large orange blotch on outer perianth segments; inner segments marked orange-brown at base; petal-like styles pinkish; mid spring to summer.

Dracunculus vulgaris
Dragon arum

Mediterranean region. Plant height to 3 ft. (90 cm). Tuber large, round. Leaves divided into five to seven lobes; base clasps flowering stem; leaf stalk pale green mottled darker green. Flower stalk whitish, mottled dull purple to black. Spathe crimson-red spathe, very dark red, or almost black on exterior, dull green inside; spathe tube 2 in. (5 cm) long, striped purple at mouth; spathe limb to 12 in. (30 cm) long, 6 in. (15 cm) wide. Spadix blackish red with long appendix, male and female flowers adjacent (not separated by sterile flowers). Fruit is scarlet berries in late summer to early fall.

Blooms early to mid summer.

Well-drained, humus-rich soil, in full sun to part shade, abundant moisture. Top-dress each spring with organic matter. Plants tolerate both water and drought in summer but increase more rapidly in moist conditions. Zone 7.

Plant 5–6 in. (12.5–15 cm) deep and 18–24 in. (45–60 cm) apart.

Use as a striking accent among other plants that complement the bold foliage. Good at the edge of a woodland.

ERANTHIS
Winter aconite

A genus of about seven species from Europe, Turkey to Afghanistan, Japan, and Siberia. The tuberous rootstock is small and irregular, with a brown skin when mature. The flowers emerge before the leaves, opening near ground level and set in a whorl of stalkless stem leaves; the stems elongate as the seed ripens. The basal leaves appear later; they are deeply divided and have stalks usually 3–5 in. (7.5–12.5 cm) long. The flowers of most species are bright yellow; they have a ring of petal-like sepals and one of petals, with prominent yellow stamens.

Dietes bicolor

Dietes grandiflora

Dracunculus vulgaris

Eranthis cilicica (International Flower Bulb Center)

Eremurus stenophyllus (International Flower Bulb Center)

Loose, humus-rich soil, ample moisture in fall and early spring. Zones 5–8.

Plant 1 in. (2.5 cm) deep, 3 in. (7.5 cm) apart, in clusters.

Use for early flowers (even before snowdrops). Plant with other early flowering spring bulbs, such as *Crocus* and *Cyclamen coum*, especially under winter-flowering shrubs such as *Hamamelis* (witch hazel). Best grown where they will not be disturbed. Light is essential, however, so planting under deciduous shrubs or trees is preferable. In old gardens, they can often be seen forming large drifts where they have seeded over the years.

Eranthis cilicica. Turkey to Afghanistan. Similar to *E. hyemalis* but more robust. Leaves finely cut, bronzy green when young. Flowers deep yellow, shiny, on short stems, only 2–3 in. (5–7.5 cm) tall, late winter.

Eranthis hyemalis. Europe. Stems to 4 in. (10 cm). Flowers bright yellow, late winter to early spring.

EREMURUS
Foxtail lily, desert candle

A genus of about 40 species from West and Central Asia (Afghanistan to India, Turkestan, Siberia, Tibet, and China). Only five or six are widely available. *Eremurus* species are among the most spectacular early summer flowering plants with a rhizomatous rootstock. The rootstock is a starfish-shaped mass of thick, fleshy roots, which must be handled with great care. The central bud from which the stem arises is large, looking much like half an egg. The tall, unbranched flower spike arises from amid a cluster of long, narrow basal leaves which may be withered by flowering time. White, yellow, or pink flowers are densely packed on the tall stem, outward-facing on short pedicels. The perianth segments of the flowers often are joined for a short distance at the base, and all open widely.

Extremely well-drained, humus-rich, sandy soil, in full sun, ample moisture in spring. Cold winters needed for good flowering.

Plant in early fall, 2–3 in. (5–7.5 cm) deep, 3 ft. (90 cm) apart.

Use as accent plants, especially against a back ground of dark foliage. The tall flower spikes can dominate a border. Excellent cut flowers.

Eremurus himalaicus. Afghanistan, Himalaya. Stems to 6 ft. (1.8 m) or more. Leaves strap-shaped, 12 in. (30 cm) or more. Flower pure white, starry, to 1 in. (2.5 cm) across, fragrant, late spring. Zones 3–8.

Eremurus ×isabellinus 'Cleopatra'. Garden hybrid (*E. stenophyllus* × *E. olgae*). Orange flower with darker red midrib on exterior of tepals and orange anther; early summer. Zones 5–8.

Eremurus robustus. Central Asia. Stems 6–10 ft. (1.8–3 m). Leaves the widest in the genus, to 4 in. (10 cm) wide, bright green. Inflorescence very long, to 4 ft. (1.2 m), crowded with many deep pink flowers; lowest flowers have long pedicels, upper ones a little shorter; early summer. Zones 6–9.

Eremurus stenophyllus (syn. *E. bungei*). Iran. Stems 2–4 ft. (60–120 cm), hairless. Leaves 12–15 in. (30–37.5 cm) long, narrow, numerous, hairless. Flowers bright yellow on pedicels several inches long, borne over three-fourths of the stem; flowers open slowly and last well, so that plants remain attractive for a long time in early summer. Zones 5–9.

ERYTHRONIUM
Dog's-tooth violet, trout lily

A genus of about 20 species distributed around the Northern Hemisphere, most from the western United States. Few spring flowers have the beauty and grace found in *Erythronium*. The Old World species *E. dens-canis* was originally called dog's-tooth violet because of its bulb, which is whitish and pointed. The rootstock is a true bulb, elongated or pointed and fleshy, stoloniferous in some species. The leaves emerge directly from the bulb (usually two per bulb), are elliptical to

Erythronium californicum 'White Beauty' (Jack Hobbs)

Erythronium dens-canis (International Flower Bulb Center)

Erythronium tuolumnense 'Pagoda'

lance-shaped, and may be plain green, spotted, or mottled, depending on the species. The single flower stalk is leafless and carries one or more flowers—seldom more than eight. The height varies according to species from 5 to 14 in. (12.5–35 cm). The flowers have six tepals, which reflex at the tips.

Blooms in spring.

Well-drained poor and rocky to humus-rich soil, depending on the species, in light shade or full sun, depending on the species, ample moisture in fall and spring.

Plant in early fall, 3 in. (7.5 cm) deep, 6 in. (15 cm) apart.

Use in front of mixed shrub borders that offer light shade, or in woodland settings. Erythroniums with spotted or mottled leaves make an attractive spring groundcover even when not in flower. In climates where they are well adapted, they should be tried on grassy slopes, and they often self-sow in gardens. For the most effective presentation, plant bulbs in groups where they can be left undisturbed.

Erythronium californicum. Fawn lily. United States. Stems to 14 in. (35 cm). Leaves richly mottled with brown, on long stalks. Flowers three or more per stem, white or cream with ring of yellow, orange, or brown at base, mid spring. Zones 4–9. **'White Beauty'**, white.

Erythronium dens-canis. Dog's-tooth violet. Europe, western Asia. Stems to 8 in. (20 cm). Leaves gray-green, heavily spotted pink and brown. Flowers solitary, strongly reflexed, white through pink to deep purple, all with a ring of red-purple at the base; anthers bluish or purplish; mid spring. Flourishes in woodland. Zones 3–9. **'Frans Hals'**, outer tepals imperial purple with greenish-bronze basal spot, inner tepals purple with greenish-yellow ring at base. **'Lilac Wonder'**, light imperial purple with chocolate-brown basal spot. **Var.** *niveum*, white flushed lavender. **'Pink Perfection'**, clear, bright pink. **'Purple King'**, large, rich purple, center spotted and striped soft brown with white margin. **'Rose Queen'**, pink. **'Snowflake'**, large pure white.

Erythronium tuolumnense. United States. Stems to 14 in. (35 cm). Leaves yellow-green, unmarked, large, surface wavy. Flowers one to four per stem, bright yellow veined green with greenish base, opening almost flat; swollen appendages at base of inner tepals; anthers yellow. Easy to cultivate; increases rapidly. Zones 4–9. **'Citronella'**, lemon yellow. **'Jeannine'**, bright sulfur yellow with brown basal ring. **'Kondo'**, mid yellow. **'Pagoda'**, pale yellow with brown basal ring, vigorous, leaves mottled. **'Sundisc'**, bright yellow, strongly mottled leaves.

Eucharis ×*grandiflora*
Amazon lily, Eucharist lily

Columbia. Bulb large, with a long neck. Stems to 2 ft. (60 cm). Leaves several, close to ground, to 20 in. (50 cm) long including long stalk, deciduous. Flowers white, slightly pendent, 5 in. (12.5 cm) across, very fragrant, five to six per stem; perianth forms a short tube and then separates into six lobes which open widely; lobes of the outer segments are narrower and longer than the inner segments; broad bases of the stamen

Eucharis ×*grandiflora* (Jack Hobbs)

form a cup reminiscent of the cup of a narcissus; anthers poised on slender filaments rising up from the cup.

Blooms in winter.

Humus-rich soil, moisture when growing. Feed with liquid organic fertilizer once growth is active. After flowering, reduce water and lower temperature, but keep humidity high during summer. Do not allow bulbs to become dry at any time. Zone 10.

Plant in spring, six bulbs to a 12-in. (30-cm) pot, covered with just enough soil to anchor the bulb and hold it upright.

Use as an elegant subject for the warm greenhouse. Can be grown with tropical orchids. An excellent cut flower and very fragrant.

EUCOMIS
Pineapple lily
A genus of about 10 species of unusual-looking plants from Africa. Related to *Scilla* and *Ornithogalum*. The bulbs are large and tunicated. The basal leaves are light green, sometimes spotted reddish, ovate, and arching back to the

Eucomis autumnalis, detail (Jack Hobbs)

Eucomis autumnalis

Eucomis comosa 'Sparkling Rose' (Jack Hobbs)

ground, where they tend to rest a bit untidily. The predominantly green flowers are closely held all around the stout, strong stems, with the characteristic tuft of bracts above them. The stamens are stubby but prominent in the center of the flowers; the perianth segments are almost equal.

Blooms summer.

Well-drained, humus-rich soil, in full sun or scattered shade, moisture during spring and early summer, less water toward end of summer. Zones 8–11.

Plant 6 in. (15 cm) deep, 12–24 in. (30–60 cm) apart.

Use in an isolated group against a background of large rocks, which brings out the subtle colors of the flowers and provides extra protection. An excellent accent plant for the front of the perennial border or for a large container. Cut flowers last for several weeks. After the flowers have faded, the seedpods—swollen green, almost triangular fruits—remain attractive.

Eucomis autumnalis. Tropical and southern Africa. Bulb globe-shaped. Stems to 18 in. (45 cm). Basal leaves 2 ft. (60 cm) long, 2–4 in. (5–10 cm) wide, with wavy margins, lax to prostrate. Crown consists of 15 to 20 bracts, 2–3 in. (5–7.5 cm) wide and 2–4 in. (5–10 cm) long. Inflorescence to 12 in. (30 cm) long; flowers 1/2 in. (12 mm) across, green fading to lighter yellow-green with age; stamens prominent in the center of the flowers; perianth segments are almost equal. **Subsp.** *amaryllidifolia*, 12 in. (30 cm) tall, leaves linear, 20 in. (50 cm) long and about 2 in. (5 cm) wide. **Subsp.** *clavata*, more robust, inflorescence cylindrical.

Eucomis comosa. South Africa. Stems lightly spotted purple, to 24 in. (60 cm). Leaves spotted purple at base and on underside, with wavy edges, 18–20 in. (45–50 cm) long. Flowers have violet-purple ovaries, light green petals that recurve slightly, throwing the stamens well out in front and showing off color of ovaries. **'Sparkling Burgundy'** has purple leaves and stem and white flowers, flushed and aging to purple.

Ferraria crispa

South Africa. Rootstock a corm, often much misshapen, without a tunic. Stems two or three per corm, to 18 in. (45 cm) but often much shorter, branched. Leaves stout, overlapping, to 12 in. (30 cm) long, shorter on the stem; uppermost leaves bractlike, surrounding the flowers. Flowers 2 in. (5 cm) or more across, borne on sturdy pedicels, velvety textured, brownish purple with greenish-white, V-shaped markings in the center; tips of segments recurved, edges very crisped; stigma brown, with the lower part surrounded by a tube formed by the anthers.

Blooms late spring to early summer.

Ferraria crispa (Jack Hobbs)

Ferraria crispa, detail (Robert Ornduff)

Well-drained soil, in full sun, moisture in spring, dry and warm in summer and fall. If soil is poor, apply fertilizer as soon as the plants appear above ground. Zone 9.

Plant 4–6 in. (10–15 cm) deep, 6–8 in. (15–20 cm) apart.

Use in rock gardens in warm climates, in bold clusters where they can enjoy the reflected warmth of the rocks. Grow where they can nestle among other low-growing plants. They tolerate salt sea spray and are easy to grow in the cool greenhouse, preferably in the ground. In a confined space, their odor may not be tolerable to those with sensitive noses.

FREESIA

A genus of about 11 species from South Africa. The round or egg-shaped corms are loosely covered by a netted tunic. Leaves are narrow and shorter than the flower stem, arranged in a fan, and continue to grow long after the flowers have finished. The flowers are on strong, branched stems, with the branch at the tip of the stem much larger than the others and bearing more flowers. The hybrids generally carry more flowers in the spike than the species, which seldom have more than four or five flowers, crowded on the stem. The flowers are all carried on one side of the stem, which bends outward just below the lowest flower, so that the flowers are held upright.

Well-drained soil, in full sun, ample moisture when growing, dry when leaves are dry. Give liquid organic fertilizer as soon as the first growth appears above ground. Zones 9–10.

Plant in fall for winter and spring flowers, in late spring for summer flowers, 2 in. (5 cm) deep, 3 in. (7.5 cm) apart.

Use as container plants, cut flowers, and for summer bedding. Florists grow them year-round in greenhouses for the cutflower and container plant markets. They make excellent house plants and are a must for warm-climate gardens, where they offer late-winter color.

Freesia 'Adonis', rose double.

Freesia 'Aphrodite', soft pink double.

Freesia 'Athene', white, good forcer.

Freesia leichtlinii. South Africa. Stems to 8 in. (20 cm), sometimes more, often much less. Leaves erect, 10 in. (25 cm). Flowers do not rise above foliage as much as in other species, very fragrant, 2 in. (5 cm) long, cream to purple, most commonly off-white or creamy, darker yellow-cream inside, purple flush on exterior; early to late spring, depending on temperature.

Freesia 'Matterhorn', huge pure white.

Freesia 'Riande', yellow, good forcer.

Freesia 'Romany', pale mauve double.

Freesia 'Rose Marie', dark pink double.

Freesia 'Royal Blue', campanula blue, white throat striped violet.

Freesia 'Matterhorn'

Freesia mixed cultivars (Jack Hobbs)

Freesia 'Stockholm'

Freesia 'Stockholm', chrysanthemum red, yellow throat.

Freesia 'Wintergold', golden.

FRITILLARIA
Fritillary

A genus of about 80 species widely distributed in the Northern Hemisphere. Closely related to *Lilium*. The stems are unbranched and bear the leaves, arranged either in whorls or in pairs. The leaves of most species are stiff and fleshy; some are glaucous. The flowers have six perianth segments, equal or nearly so, called tepals. Each tepal has a nectary at the base, which may be conspicuously depressed (forming a ridge on the "outside" of the flower) or contrastingly colored. There are six stamens and a single style, sometimes divided into two at the tip and as long as the stamens. The flowers range from narrowly

Freesia 'Wintergold'

Fritillaria acmopetala

tubular to almost flat, but most are bell-shaped. The fruit is a capsule (winged in some species, unwinged in others) with numerous flat, winged seeds. In some species, all parts of the plant have an unpleasant "foxy" odor, especially noticeable as the leaves emerge.

Well-drained, humus-rich soil, in light shade. Give weak feedings of organic fertilizer in fall and when leaves emerge. Hardiness depends on the species.

Plant in fall, with a depth of soil equal to three times the height of the bulb, and spaced apart by about four times the bulb's diameter.

Use up close where the subtle flower colors are best appreciated, such as in the rock garden or in small-scale plantings among shrubs. The crown imperial (*Fritillaria imperialis*) is a popular early spring subject in the perennial border. Enthusiasts cultivate the more difficult species in bulb frames and alpine houses, where their specialized moisture regimes can be followed.

Fritillaria acmopetala. Turkey, Cyprus, Syria, Lebanon. Stems 12–30 in. (30–75 cm). Leaves narrow, to 3 in. (7.5 cm) long, alternate on stem. Flowers solitary, sometimes up to three, bell-shaped with tips strongly curled back, olive green with reddish brown blotches or bands on outside, shining olive green within; mid spring. Easy in ordinary garden soils, increasing rapidly. Many plants grown under other names are in fact this species. Zones 7–10.

Fritillaria biflora. Chocolate lily, mission bells. United States. Stems to 6–12 in. (15–30 cm). Leaves shiny green, large, mostly basal. Flowers up to 12, not reflexed, dark brown, often marked with green, mid spring. Zones 7–9. **'Martha Roderick'**, robust, brownish-red flowers marked cream or green on exterior.

Fritillaria bucharica. Afghanistan, Central Asia. Stems to 12 in. (30 cm). Leaves paired on lower stem, remainder alternate; prominent pair of bracts under each flower. Flowers white with

Fritillaria imperialis 'Aurora'

Fritillaria imperialis 'Aurora', detail

Fritillaria imperialis 'Lutea'

Fritillaria pallidiflora

Fritillaria persica 'Adiyaman'

green veins, numerous, early spring. Requires dry summer and protection from spring frosts. Zones 5–9.

Fritillaria glauca. Siskiyou lily. United States. Stems to 5 in. (12.5 cm). Leaves lance-shaped, glaucous. Flowers yellow, sometimes spotted brown, rarely entirely dark brown, mid spring. Not too difficult to grow when given a dry summer. Zones 6–8.

Fritillaria imperialis. Crown imperial. Asia. Bulbs very large, malodorous. Stems 2–4 ft. (60–120 cm). Leaves shiny green, in whorls. Flowers pendent in an umbel below a distinctive tuft of large green bracts, large, broadly bell-shaped, bright orange with pale raised nectaries, scented of rotting meat; mid spring. A very showy plant for gardens, tolerating a wide range of well-drained soils in full sun. Leave plantings undisturbed. Zones 4–7. **'Aureomarginata'**, leaves with pale yellow margins. **'Aurora'**, a strong grower with orange-red flowers. **'Lutea'**, yellow. **'Lutea Maxima'**, a more robust yellow form. **'Prolifera'**, two whorls of flowers. **'Rubra'**, brownish orange. **'Sulpherino'**, pale orange with yellow margin.

Fritillaria meleagris. Snake's head fritillary, guinea-hen flower, leper lily. Europe, Russia. Stems wiry, to 15 in. (37.5 cm). Leaves generally four to six, narrow, slightly glaucous, alternate. Flowers pale pink to purple, strongly checkered inside; white forms common, showing greenish checkering; mid spring. Plant only where moisture is present year-round. Tolerates dappled shade and likes soil high in organic matter. Zones 4–9. **'Aphrodite'**, large white. **'Artemis'**, checkered purple and green. **'Charon'**, light purple checkered with black. **'Orion'**, dull purple. **'Saturnus'**, bright reddish violet.

Fritillaria michailovskyi. Turkey. Stems to 9 in. (22.5 cm), usually shorter. Flowers dark purple with prominent yellow tips, mid spring. Widely offered and easy to grow in climates with a dry spring. Zones 7–9.

Fritillaria micrantha. United States. Stems to 3 ft. (90 cm). Flowers very small, greenish yellow to buff, faintly checkered, mid spring. Zone 8.

Fritillaria persica

Fritillaria pallidiflora. Central Asia, China, Siberia. Stems stout, 10–30 in. (25–75 cm). Leaves glaucous, broad, alternate or opposite. Flowers pale greenish yellow, very lightly checkered reddish brown inside, mid spring. Zones 3–8.

Fritillaria persica. Persian lily. Turkey, Iran. Stems to 45 in. (112.5 cm). Leaves glaucous, lance-shaped, alternate, sometimes slightly twisted. Flowers numerous, more than 30 on a well-grown plant, dark plum-purple to gray-green, widely conical, mid spring. An interesting accent among other spring bulbs. Persists only in well-drained soil in regions with hot, dry summers. Zones 5–9. **'Adiyaman'** is a robust selection named for the town in Turkey near which is was found.

Fritillaria pontica. Greece, Turkey. Stems 15–30 in. (37.5–75 cm). Leaves elliptical-lance-shaped, lower opposite, upper in whorl. Flowers green flushed brown, bell-shaped, not check-ered, one to four on stalk, mid spring. Zone 6.

Fritillaria pudica. Johnny-jump-up, yellow bell. United States and Canada. Stems to 10 in. (25 cm), usually shorter. Leaves narrow, bright green, near base of stem. Flowers conical, mostly one to three per stem, golden yellow, flushed darker at base, aging to orange, mid spring. Re-quires moderately dry winter, dry summer. Zone 3.

GALANTHUS
Snowdrop
A genus of 18 species from Europe and West Asia. Related to *Leucojum*, but segments are of different lengths (those of *Leucojum* are of equal length). The bulbs are round and have brown tunics. Each bulb produces three leaves; two of these lengthen, and the third remains short, sheathing the bases of the longer leaves and the flower stem. The leaves may be absent, 1 or 2 in. (2.5–5 cm) long, or nearly full length at flowering time, depending on the species. The flowers are white, variously marked with green. The shape of the green blotches or stripes is an important means of identification. The flower has a teardrop shape when closed in dark-ness or dull weather; when the sun comes out, the outer segments flare more or less widely. The three outer segments are longer than the inner three; the latter are notched at the tip. The flowers are usually solitary, covered by a spathe in bud and drooping when fully developed.

Blooms in early spring or fall, depending on the species.

Galanthus nivalis (International Flower Bulb Center)

Humus-rich soil, in part sun, moisture when growing.

Plant 2–3 in. (5–7.5 cm) deep, 4–5 in. (10–12.5 cm) apart.

Use in masses at the edge of woodland or in front of shady borders. Established clumps have a lot of foliage which must be left to wither in early summer. Can be grown in containers, brought indoors to enjoy. Makes long-lasting cut flowers. Most species are sweetly fragrant, though this often goes unnoticed because they flower in such cold weather.

Galanthus elwesii. Giant snowdrop. Bulgaria, Greece, Ukraine, Turkey, Yugoslavia. Stems to 10 in. (25 cm). Leaves gray-green, developing to over 1 in. (2.5 cm) wide after flowering. Inner segments variably marked with an inverted V, an arch, or an inverted heart near the tip, sometimes an inverted V at the base which may be joined to the V at the tip; green at the base and tip, but this color is variable and often will appear suffused throughout the inner segments. Plants grown under the name G. *caucasicus* are almost all G. *elwesii*; small plants with narrow, glaucous leaves grown as G. *elwesii* are probably G. *gracilis*. Zones 6–9.

Galanthus ikariae. Aegean Islands. Stems 3–8 in. (7.5–20 cm). Leaves broad, dark matte green, recurving when mature, one wider than the other and overlapping it. Inner perianth segments have a bold arch-shaped mark, sometimes flat-topped, over one-half to two-thirds of their length, and a similar mark inside. Confused in cultivation with G. *woronowii*, which has bright, shiny green leaves. Zones 6–9.

Galanthus nivalis. Common snowdrop. Europe, Ukraine. Stems 3–8 in. (7.5–20 cm). Leaves slightly glaucous, linear, widening slightly in one-third their length, erect or somewhat curled back, not wrapping one around the other, margins flat and often slightly turned under. Inner segments marked with a narrow arch shape or an inverted V shape, the ends of which are usually enlarged; inner surface has a mark extending to the base. Mid to late winter, sometimes into spring, depending on the variety. Zones 4–9. **'Lutescens'** (syn. 'Sandersii'), inner segments tipped yellow,

ovary yellow. **Forma** *pleniflorus* **'Lady Elphinstone'**, inner perianth segments marked yellow. **Forma** *pleniflorus* **'Pusey Green Tip'**, outer and inner segments tipped green. **'Poculiformis'**, inner and outer segments about equal in length and unmarked. **'Sam Arnott'**, robust, with large flowers. **'Scharlockii'**, an enlarged, leaflike spathe that looks like two erect leaves.

Galtonia candicans
Summer hyacinth

South Africa and Lesotho. Bulbs large, with thin tunics. Stems to 50 in. (125 cm). Leaves pale green, to 2 in. (5 cm) wide and 30 in. (75 cm)

Galtonia candicans (Jack Hobbs)

long, tapering gradually to a fine point, sometimes erect but usually curled back. Flowers slightly fragrant, held in a loose raceme, up to 40 per stem, 2 in. (5 cm) long, pendent, white (sometimes with green tips and base), on pedicels over 2 in. (5 cm) long.

Blooms in summer.

Well-drained soil, in full sun, moisture during spring and summer. No staking needed. Give weak feedings of liquid fertilizer as soon as growth is seen in the spring and discontinue as the flower stems emerge. Zones 5–9.

Plant in late winter, with the tops just below the surface of the soil, 18–24 in. (45–60 cm) apart.

Use in groups of five or more. The flowers remain attractive for six weeks. Galtonia grows well in large containers.

Geranium tuberosum (International Flower Bulb Center)

Geranium tuberosum
Cranesbill

Mediterranean region and east to Iran. Rootstock tuberous. Stems 8–16 in. (20–40 cm). Leaves dark green, very finely cut and feathery; upper leaves stalkless and in pairs. Flowers to 1½ in. (4 cm) across, bright rosy purple with darker veins, deep blue anthers, and crimson stigma; petals notched and widest at tips. The flowers have five sepals and five petals, overlapping and equal in size. There are 10 stamens, more or less united at the base, held in two whorls, the outer whorl located opposite the petals and the inner one opposite the sepals. After pollination, the base of the style grows, forming the long beak for which the genus is named cranesbill. This beak slowly dries and splits into five strips, which curl and fling the seeds away from the plant.

Well-drained, humus-rich soil, in full sun to light shade. Zones 8–10.

Plant 2 in. (5 cm) deep, 10–14 in. (25–35 cm) apart.

Use to introduce bright spring color to dry shade; the foliage makes a good groundcover through winter but is dormant in summer. Easy to grow, robust (though sometimes invasive), and attractive.

'Leonidas', more robust and larger-flowered. Leaves appear in fall and wither soon after flowering in late spring.

GLADIOLUS
Sword lily

A genus of up to 250 species and thousands of named hybrids, distributed in southern and tropical Africa, and from southwestern Europe and the Mediterranean coastal regions east to central Asia. The base of the stem is swollen, forming a corm. The leaves are always sword-shaped. The flower spike is often one-sided. The tube formed by the perianth segments is curved. In many species, the flowers open wide; in garden hybrids, they are not so open and are more crowded on the stem.

Well-drained, humus-rich, sandy soil, in full sun.

Plant in spring, at least 4–6 in. (10–15 cm) deep, about 6–10 in. (15–25 cm) apart; miniature hybrids and species may be planted less deeply.

Use as a striking accent among annuals and in perennial borders. Their proportions make them difficult to integrate tastefully, but choosing cultivars with smaller flowers and placing them in groups among other tall plants helps. They do well in containers, but must be carefully selected for this purpose because plants can become quite heavy when in full bloom. Gladioli make good cut flowers; for long-lasting cut flowers, cut stems as soon as the first buds show color.

Gladiolus 'Candy Stripe'

Gladiolus communis

Gladiolus 'Candy Stripe'. Flowers creamy white, wavy edge, with reddish stripes in the throat.

Gladiolus communis. Saint John's lily. Spain, Italy, North Africa, Corsica, Malta. Stems to 2 ft. (60 cm), usually less. Leaves three to five, in a basal fan. Flowers to 15 per spike, bright burgundy red, 2–3 in. (5–7.5 cm) long, facing in two or three directions but not all around the stem; late spring to early summer. Zones 6–10.

Gladiolus dalenii (syn. *G. primulinus*). Parrot lily. South Africa to Ethiopia. Corm 2 in. (5 cm) across. Stems strong, 4–5 ft. (1.2–1.5 m). Leaves usually four, narrow, to 30 in. (75 cm). Flowers often more than 20 per two-sided spike, yellow, orange, red, pink, or purple, often striped and mottled with another color; late summer. Upper three segments form a hood; uppermost is much larger than the other two upper segments. Lower three segments narrower, often with a patch of yellow at the tips. Zone 9.

Gladiolus murielae (syn. *Acidanthera bicolor*). Ethiopia, Tanzania, Malawi, and Mozambique. Corm globose. Stems to 36 in. (90 cm). Leaves sword-shaped. Flowers white, long-tubed, 3 in. (7.5 cm) or more in diameter, with distinct purple spot at base of segments; flowers carried in two ranks, usually six to eight per stem. Fragrant at night, reportedly to attract long-tongued hawk moths. Flowering late summer.

Gladiolus tristis. Marsh Afrikaner. South Africa. Stems to 40 in. (100 cm) but usually around 24 in. (60 cm). Leaves three or four, more or less cylindrical. Flowers 3 in. (7.5 cm) across, up to 15 per spike, rarely more, very fragrant at night, green and brown; summer. **Var.** *concolor*, pale yellow. A popular garden plant. Appreciates moisture year-round. Zones 7–10.

Gladiolus virescens. South Africa. Stems 5–10 in. (12.5–25 cm). Flowers yellow closely striped with brown, spring. Zone 9.

Gloriosa superba

Africa and India. Tubers long, fleshy, white, multiplying quickly. Leaves with tendrils. Stems light green, looking fragile though they are not. Stamens prominent in the center of strongly reflexed tepals.

Gladiolus dalenii

Gladiolus murielae (Jack Hobbs)   *Gladiolus tristis* (Jack Hobbs)

Gloriosa superba 'Rothschildiana', detail (International Flower Bulb Center)

Gloriosa superba 'Rothschildiana' (Jack Hobbs)

A peculiar characteristic is that the stigma bends at a right angle as it leaves the ovary. Perianth segments yellow, orange, red, or bicolored with zones of these colors; often crinkled along the edges, and, even when fully reflexed, the tips sometimes curl back. All parts of the plant are poisonous.

Blooms summer.

Well-drained soil, in full sun, moisture to get them growing, after which they tolerate drier conditions. They grow and flower best where they are moist through the growing period. In winter, keep them dry. Provide support on which the plants can scramble upward. Zones 9–12.

Plant 1–2 in. (2.5–5 cm) deep.

Use in the cool greenhouse and for long-lasting cut flowers. Much in demand among florists. Must be grown in large containers to leave room for expansion. Adds an exotic touch to the mild-climate garden.

'Rothschildiana', a popular selections, bright red flowers with crinkled edges, yellow margins, and a yellow basal zone that disappears as the flower ages, borne on stalks to 4 in. (10 cm) long.

HEMEROCALLIS
Daylily

A genus of about 15 species from East Asia and Central Europe. Most have fibrous roots, more or less thickened; a few are distinctly tuberous. Over the years the genus has received much attention from hybridizers, and few true species are found in gardens today. The common name aptly describes the flowers which last only one or two days. The foliage is basal, grasslike, and up to 4 ft. (1.2 m) long in robust plants. The flower stalks are sturdy and carry the flowers well above the foliage. Most attain about 3 ft. (90 cm) in height, but a few reach 6 ft. (1.8 m). The genus can be divided into two groups: plants with an open, branched inflorescence, and those in which the flowers are held close together with a distinct, broad bract below them. The flowers are trumpet-

Hemerocallis 'King Porcelain' (Klehm's Song Sparrow Perennial)

Hemerocallis 'Real Purple Star' (Klehm's Song Sparrow Perennial)

shaped. The most common colors are yellow, orange, or reddish purple.

Any garden soil, in full sun, moisture in summer. In poor soils, give a spring feeding of a slow-release balanced fertilizer. Zones 4–9.

Plant year-round, with base of the leaves at the soil surface, about 1 ft. (30 cm) apart if low growing, 1½–3 ft. (45–90 cm) apart if taller growing.

Use in borders, with other perennials, as bold beds in lawns, or as groundcover (for example, to line driveways). Few plants are as easy to grow or as tolerant of such a wide range of garden conditions. Many species and some hybrids are sweetly fragrant. About their only flaw is that individual flowers last such a short time.

Hemerocallis 'August Flame', red with a yellow throat.

Hemerocallis 'Bald Eagle'; rich crimson.

Hemerocallis 'Catherine Woodbery', pink with a chartreuse throat.

Hemerocallis 'King Porcelain', pinkish with a green throat

Hemerocallis 'Moonlight Masquerade', cream with a purple eye.

Hemerocallis 'Pardon Me', deep red.

Hemerocallis 'Real Purple Star', medium purple with a yellowish throat and white margin.

Hemerocallis 'Satin Clouds', cream with a bright yellow throat.

Hemerocallis 'Stella d'Oro', golden yellow. A favorite of landscape architects.

Hemerocallis 'Strawberry Candy', pink, with rosy band and a green throat.

HIPPEASTRUM
Amaryllis, knight's star lily

A genus of about 80 species from South America. Formerly classified as *Amaryllis* and best known by this name. The three important categories of cultivars are large-flowered singles, large-flowered doubles, and miniatures. The bulb of most species is large and globe-shaped. The flowers are funnel-shaped and borne in an umbel on a stout, cylindrical, hollow, leafless stem which may be coated with a waxy bloom. Large bulbs may produce more than one flowering stem. The three inner perianth segments are often narrower than the three outer ones. The stamens also are of unequal length and have the peculiar habit of bending down and then curving upward. The stigma remains below the stamens and usually is much longer, often equal to the length of the perianth segments. The flowers are typically large—over 4 in. (10 cm) long and as much as 8–10 in. (20–25 cm) across in the largest hybrids. The leaves generally appear after the flowers or are partly developed at flowering; they are bright or dark green, broadly strap-shaped and somewhat fleshy.

Humus-rich soil, in full sun, moisture when growing but not wet. After flowering, cut off the flowers, but leave the stem and foliage. Feed weekly for six to eight weeks with an organic liquid fertilizer. Reduce water in July, and stop watering completely in August. leaves often stay green if watering continues; then the bulbs do not go dormant, and the chance of flowering the following year is greatly diminished. Zones 9–10.

Plant in fall, one-third of bulb above soil level.

Use as an indoor plant, brought into flower in December. Can be grown outside where night temperatures during the growing season do not drop below about 40°F (4°C).

Hippeastrum 'Apple Blossom'. Flowers pinkish white.

Hippeastrum 'Masai'. Flowers white with red stripes.

Hippeastrum papilio. Butterfly amaryllis. Brazil. Stems to 2 ft. (60 cm). Leaves evergreen. Flowers cream to pale green with conspicuous reddish-brown veins and streaks; upper three tepals heavily marked in center with veins toward margin; spring.

Hippeastrum 'Apple Blossom'

Hippeastrum papilio

Hippeastrum hybrids

White-flowered *Hippeastrum* hybrids in a garden bed with blue-flowered delphiniums

HOMERIA
Cape tulip

A genus of about 32 species from South Africa and extending into Namibia, Botswana, and Lesotho. The rootstock is a corm. The basal leaves are usually solitary, but sometimes two or three are produced, and the flower stalk also carries several leaves. The six similarly-shaped perianth segments that make up the flowers are not fused but come together at the base to form a cup. They then spread out flat. The stamens are erect.

Well-drained soil, in full sun or light shade, moderate moisture when growing, dry after flowering. Zones 9–12.

Plant in spring, 1 in. (2.5 cm) deep, 3–4 in. (7.5–10 cm) apart.

Use in masses in the sunny border where their unusual form and colors can be appreciated. They are light and airy in effect, and also make good container plants. In favorable climates, they naturalize rapidly by self-sowing.

Homeria collina. Corm has dark, coarse, fibrous tunic. Stems to 18 in. (45 cm). Leaves thin

Homeria collina

and arching, often lax. Flowers numerous in long succession, about 2 in. (5 cm) across, light salmon orange to deep yellow; flowering in spring from fall planting, later in summer from spring-planted corms.

Homeria pallida. Yellow tulip. Stems to 2 ft. (60 cm). Leaves and fruit poisonous. Flowers light yellow, spotted crimson at base, sweetly scented; late spring.

HYACINTHOIDES
Bluebell

A genus of three species assigned down through the years to *Scilla*, *Agraphis*, *Endymion*, and now *Hyacinthoides*. The common name of the most familiar species, however, is constant: English bluebell. May it be forever unchanged! The plants are a lovely sight in the English countryside in April and May. The true bulb is composed of tubular scales and has the unusual character-istic of being renewed annually. The flowers are borne in an erect raceme on pedicels of moderate length, with two bracts below each flower. They are bell-shaped and blue-lavender, though white and pink forms are common. The leaves are narrowly strap-shaped and shiny green.

Leafy, humus-rich soil, in light shade, with a wide range of moisture needs. Zone 5.

Plant in spring, at least 4 in. (10 cm) deep in heavy soil, 6–8 in. (15–20 cm) deep in light soil, 4–6 in. (10–15 cm) apart.

Use in open, deciduous woodland, where the drifts of flowers look splendid in spring. Often used as a border for spring-flowering shrubs such as rhododendrons and azaleas. Always plant them in large quantities and leave them undisturbed for years.

Hyacinthoides hispanica. Spanish bluebell. Iberian Peninsula. Stems 8–20 in. (20–50 cm). Leaves fleshy, strap-shaped, produced with flowers,

Hyacinthoides hispanica (Jack Hobbs)

Hyacinthoides non-scripta mass planting under trees

Hyacinthoides non-scripta as accent plants

to 2 ft. (60 cm), about 1 in. (2.5 cm) wide. Flowers to 15 or more per stem, bell-shaped, nearly ¾ in. (2 cm) long; anthers blue; spring. **'Alba'**, white. **'Arnold Prinsen'**, robust, pink. **'Blue Bird'**, early, dark blue. **'Blue Queen'**, later, lighter blue. **'Excelsior'**, violet-blue with marine-blue edge. **'Rose Queen'**, clear pink. **'Sky Blue'**, later, dark blue. **'White Triumphator'**, robust, white.

Hyacinthoides italica. Italian bluebell. France, Italy, Spain, Portugal. Stems 4–12 in. (10–30 cm). Leaves usually four to eight, 6–8 in. (15–20 cm) long, ¼–½ in. (6–12 mm) wide. Flowers to 20 per stem, lightly fragrant, to ½ in. (12 mm) across, pale to deep blue, spring. Lower flowers have longer pedicels than the upper, producing a cone-shaped raceme.

Hyacinthoides non-scripta. English bluebell. Europe. Stems to 18 in. (45 cm), bending over at the tip. Flowers fragrant, usually carried on one side of the stem, midblue, spring. White and pink forms exist.

Hyacinthus orientalis
Common hyacinth

Eastern Mediterranean. Stems to 12 in. (30 cm). Leaves four to six, almost 1 in. (2.5 cm) wide, bright green, with distinct hooks at the tips. Flowers to 15 widely scattered on the stem, may be white, yellow, mauve, or blue-lavender; extremely fragrant, almost 1 in. (2.5 cm) long; tepals open wide to an almost starry flower.

Blooms early to mid spring.

Well-drained, sandy soil, in full sun. Zones 5–9.

Plant in fall, 3–5 in. (7.5–12.5 cm) deep in mild areas, 8 in. (20 cm) deep in warmest areas, 6–9 in. (15–22.5 cm) apart.

Use where the fragrance can be enjoyed, perhaps by a door or window. Hybrids are much used in the florist trade because they are easy to force and grow and have a good "shelf life" while in flower. Home gardeners can force them for the holiday season. Small bulbs ok for outdoor planting, but larger bulbs best for forcing indoors.

Hyacinthus orientalis 'Gipsy Queen'

Hyacinthus orientalis 'L'Innocence' (International Flower Bulb Center)

Hyacinthus orientalis 'Pink Pearl'

'**Carnegie**', pure white, very fragrant.

'**City of Haarlem**', yellow.

'**Gipsy Queen**', salmon-orange.

'**Jan Bos**', red.

'**L'Innocence**', pure white.

Multiflora hyacinths, several few-flowered stems from one bulb.

'**Pink Pearl**', bright pink.

Roman hyacinths, sometimes called "var. *albulus*," smaller-flowered than the type.

Ipheion uniflorum
Spring starflower

Argentina. True bulbs white. Stems to 6 in. (15 cm). Leaves linear, flat, pale green. Flowers light to deep violet, rarely white, sweetly fragrant, one per stem, borne on a 1-in. (2.5-cm) pedicel enclosed by a papery bract; perianth tube short; lobes open flat; stamens within the tube. Very easy to grow.

Blooms winter to spring.

Well-drained soil, with dappled shade during the hottest part of the day, moisture needed in spring and early summer. Give a general fertilizer in spring as soon as the leaves show. Zones 6–10.

Plant in fall, 2 in. (5 cm) deep, 3–5 in. (7.5–12.5 cm) apart.

Use on the sunny side of a wooded area. It is invasive in mild-climate gardens and is good for filling in among shrubs that are not too dense. Once established, the clumps can smother weeds. Flowers are not showy enough to warrant their use as container plants.

'**Froyle Mill**', violet.

'**Violaceum**', almost white flowers with deep blue midrib.

'**Wisley Blue**', large pale blue.

Ipheion uniflorum 'Wisley Blue' (Jack Hobbs)

IRIS
Flag, sword lily

A genus of more than 300 species throughout the Northern Hemisphere. Irises are divided into two main groups based on their roots. In the bulbous group are Juno, Reticulata, and Dutch irises. In the rhizomatous group are Bearded, Beardless, and Evansia (or Crested) irises. The perianth tube branches into inner ("standards") and outer ("falls") series of three segments each. These segments surround the style column, which also branches into three. Each branch bears on its underside the stigmatic lip, usually near the tip; above the lip, it splits into two stigmatic crests. These style branches are usually arched and concave, as if protecting the anthers that lie beneath them. In some species, a "beard" or tuft of many fine hairs occurs on the central upper part of the falls. Most species have a contrastingly colored blotch near the base of the falls; it is called the "signal patch" and is believed to guide pollinating insects to the hidden anthers. The leaves are sword-shaped and stiff.

Blooms spring to summer.

Soil, light, and moisture requirements variable. Most irises prefer full sun. Do not cut the leaves short after flowering; rather, allow them to complete their natural growth cycle before tidying up the plants.

Plant in mid summer, with roots firmed in soil but top of rhizome exposed to the sun, 8–12 in. (20–30 cm) apart. Plant bulbous types in fall, 3 in. (7.5 cm) deep, 4 in. (10 cm) apart.

Use bulbous irises for cut flowers. They grow well in containers.

Iris bucharica

Iris 'Bronze Beauty' (Dutch). Stems 18–24 in. (45–60 cm); leaves dark blue-green; flowers two or three per stem, standards light heliotrope-violet, falls dark violet, both flushed cinnamon brown near margins, fragrant, late spring, vigorous.

Iris bucharica (Juno). Central Asia. Stems to 18 in. (45 cm). Leaves shiny green, 8–12 in. (20–30 cm) long, to 2 in. (5 cm) wide. Flowers to seven per stem, slightly fragrant; falls golden yellow or creamy white, with large golden blotch at the tip, to 1 in. (2.5 cm) wide; standards white or light yellow; early spring. A robust plant, good for the rock garden or raised bed. Plant with the neck of the bulb just at the soil surface. Take great care not to break or detach the fingerlike roots; though the plant can grow on without them, it will not be as strong for several years. Zones 5–9.

Iris cycloglossa (Juno). Afghanistan. Stems to 12 in. (30 cm) in the wild, to 3 ft. (90 cm) in cultivation. Leaves usually six, narrow, to 12 in. (30 cm) long. Flowers to eight per stem, with narrow falls, 6 in. (15 cm) across, clove-scented, lilac; late spring to early summer. Requires some moisture in summer.

Iris danfordiae (International Flower Bulb Center)

Iris danfordiae (Reticulata). Turkey. Stems to 4 in. (10 cm). Leaves short at flowering time, later to 12 in. (30 cm), solitary, compact, rounded, bright yellow, slightly fragrant; standards much reduced; haft (the narrow, basal part) of falls dotted with bright yellowish green or orange; late winter. See *I. reticulata* for cultivation.

Iris ensata (Beardless) (syn. *I. kaempferia*). Japanese iris. Japan, China, Korea, Russia. Stems 2–3 ft. (60–90 cm), often branched. Leaves to 2 ft. (60 cm), stiff, erect. Flowers usually two per branch; mainly in early summer. Wild forms have falls 3 in. (7.5 cm) long, standards a little shorter, and are usually deep red-purple. Hundreds of selections, many with wide, ruffled falls; color range includes white, all shades of red-purple and blue-lavender, bicolors, strongly veined and spotted falls. Very showy flowers—some selections to 10 in. (25 cm) across. Use near or in shallow water. Zones 5–8.

Iris germanica (Bearded). Common iris. Mediterranean region, wild origin uncertain. Stems 2–3 ft. (60–90 cm), branching. Leaves sword-shaped, 18 in. (45 cm) or more, 1–1½ in. (2.5–4 cm) wide. Flowers one on each of two branches, fragrant; falls bright purple, reflexed at midpoint, yellow beard; standards erect, often slightly paler than falls. **Var.** *florentina* has white flowers with traces of blue and is said to be the fleur-de-lis of French heraldry; it is also known commonly as the Florentine iris.

Iris histrioides (Reticulata). Turkey. Stems to 10 in. (25 cm). Leaves very short at flowering. Flowers blue, to 3 in. (7.5 cm) across. See *I. reticulata* for cultivation. **'Angel's Eye'**, pure blue. **'Major'**, deep blue falls with white spots. **Var.** *sophenensis*, narrow segments, deep violet-blue with yellow ridge on falls.

Iris japonica (Evansia). Orchid iris. Japan, China. Stems to 2 ft. (60 cm), with erect

Iris ensata (Jack Hobbs)

Iris ensata 'The Geisha' (Jack Hobbs)

Iris germanica

branches. Leaves held in fanlike tuft, sword-shaped, dark green. Flowers lavender-violet, about 1 in. (2.5 cm) across; falls cut irregularly, spotted yellow and white in center; petal-like crests fringed. Well-drained, humus-rich soil, moisture in summer. Zones 8–10. Use for long-blooming flowers in subtropical climates.

Iris latifolia 'King of the Blues'. Flowers dark blue, early summer.

Iris nusairiensis (Juno). Syria. Stems to 4 in. (10 cm). Flowers white or blue with purple veins around yellow crest.

Iris pallida (Bearded). Dalmatian iris. Europe. Stems 2–3 ft. (60–90 cm). Spathes papery. Flowers pale lilac blue to violet, very fragrant, late spring. Zones 5–9. 'Aurea Variegata', yellow-striped leaves.

Iris pseudacorus (Beardless). Fleur-de-lis, yellow flag. Europe to western Asia. Stems 24–70 in. (60–175 cm). Flowers bright yellow with brown or violet markings on falls, and darker

Iris pseudacorus

Iris japonica

Iris ensata 'Variegata' (foreground) and *I. pallida* 'Aurea Variegata' (background)

Iris pseudacorus 'Variegata' (Jack Hobbs)

yellow zone, late spring to mid summer. Use in shallow water. **'Alba'**, white. **'Bastardii'**, pale yellow without darker blotch. **'Golden Fleece'**, golden yellow. **'Variegata'**, leaves longitudinally striped.

Iris reticulata (Reticulata). Caucasus, Turkey, Iraq, Iran. Stems 6–8 in. (15–20 cm). Leaves two to four, square in cross section with four ribs, as high as flowers at flowering time but up to 12 in. (30 cm) later. Flowers solitary, deep blue mauve; falls with raised orange ridge bordered in white; standards erect. Plant bulbs 2–3 in. (5–7.5 cm) deep, 2–3 in. (5–7.5 cm) apart, in very well-drained, gritty soil in a site where they can dry out in summer. Use in rock gardens and containers. Zones 3–9.

Iris **'Stitch in Time'** (Bearded). Stems 18–24 in. (45–60 cm).

Iris unguicularis (Beardless). Algerian iris. Mediterranean region. Stems to 10 in. (25 cm). Leaves narrow, evergreen. Flowers pale to rich lavender, very sweetly scented; crest orange. Slightly alkaline soil. Zones 7–10. **Subsp. *carica* f. *angustifolia***, small lilac-blue flowers, center of falls and base of standards white. **Subsp. *cretensis***, small flowers, standards purple-blue, falls white veined violet and striped orange in center, mid spring. **'Walter Butt'**, pale lavender, large, mid winter.

Iris versicolor (Beardless). Blue flag. Canada, United States. Stems 18–24 in. (45–60 cm). Flowers lavender, violet, blue-violet, red-purple, rarely white; falls have central yellowish blotch surrounded by white zone veined with purple; standards slightly smaller than falls; late spring. Use in shallow water or in very moist soil. Zones 4–9. **Var. *arkeonensis***, blue with violet spots. **Var. *kermesina*** (syn. 'Kermesina'), reddish purple. **Var. *rosea***, pink.

Iris **'White Excelsior'** (Dutch). Stems 18–20 in. (45–50 cm); flowers white with a yellow spot, late spring.

Iris reticulata
(International Flower
Bulb Center)

Iris 'White
Excelsior'
(International
Flower Bulb
Center)

IXIA
Wand flower, corn lily

A genus of about 50 species from South Africa, with small corms and fibrous tunics. The flower stalks may be branched or not. The leaves are narrow, sword-shaped, and tough, held erect or nearly so; generally there are only three to five leaves per corm, and a few small leaves on the flowering stem. The stems range from a few inches to over 20 in. (50 cm) in height. Most species produce many flowers per stem, often more than 20. The flowers are showy. All have a fairly long, slender perianth tube. The lobes flare to produce a saucer-shaped, bowl-shaped, or flat flower. There are six perianth segments, or tepals, and three stamens. The stamens arise from the perianth tube and are shorter than the segments but prominent. The tube is usually darker than the lobes, so that a dark zone appears in the center of the flower. Plants that feature a third zone of color between this dark center and the main color of the lobes are called "tricolored."

Blooms spring to early summer, depending on the species.

Well-drained soil, in sun, but afternoon shade preserves the delicate flower colors where temperatures are above 90°F (32°C), moisture in fall and winter. Zones 9–10.

Plant in fall, 1–2 in. (2.5–5 cm) deep, 3–4 in. (7.5–10 cm) apart.

Use in groups of at least 15 to 20 for a blaze of color in late spring and early summer, continuing after the late tulips. They multiply easily, and once a bed is established, the gardener will not need to purchase more corms. I have seen beds of these plants accidentally rototilled, and the following year the number of flowers was startling. Anyone who likes bright, cheerful colors should try ixias. A must for gardens in a Mediterranean cli-

Ixia cultivars (Jack Hobbs)

mate. As container plants, they provide excellent color, in flower for a month or more, but must be given the brightest light possible.

Ixia '**Blue Bird**', white with deep blue center and reverse.

Ixia campanulata. Stems 6–12 in. (15–30 cm). Flowers dark purple lilac to dark crimson, spring.

Ixia '**Giant**', white with purple center and tips.

Ixia '**Hogarth**', large creamy yellow with purple center.

Ixia longituba. Stems 14–28 in. (35–45 cm). Flowers pink to white, spring.

Ixia '**Marquette**', bright yellow with purplish-red center and tips.

Ixia '**Rose Emperor**', rose pink with deeper center.

Ixiolirion tataricum
Blue lily

Stems to 18 in. (45 cm), usually less. Leaves basal, generally three to eight. Flowers in an umbel, violet-blue, with three darker veins in each tepal. Tepals to 2 in. (5 cm) long, spreading, sometimes curled back.

Blooms late spring to early summer.

Well-drained soil, in full sun, with moisture from late fall through early spring. Requires a hot, dry summer dormancy to flourish. Needs little or no feeding in the garden. Zones 5–9.

Plant in late summer or early fall, 6 in. (15 cm) deep, 6–10 in. (15–25 cm) apart. The leaves emerge in winter and can be damaged by frost.

Use in the front of a sunny border or in protected pockets in the rock garden, though the plants are rather tall and slender for the latter use. A good cut flower.

Kniphofia uvaria
Red-hot poker

South Africa. Rootstock is a mass of short, thick rhizomes with the junction of stem and root at soil level or just below it. Stems to 3 ft. (90 cm). Leaves V-shaped in cross section, tough, often slightly toothed near tips, to 30 in. (75 cm) long. Inflorescence resembles a fireplace poker, the

Ixiolirion tataricum

lowest flowers on the stem opening first. Flower color brilliant scarlet or greenish tinged red in bud, opening orange or greenish yellow.

Blooms late spring into summer or fall.

Well-drained, humus-rich soil, in full sun, moist while leaves are green. No feeding is necessary, but a spring application of balanced fertilizer is appreciated. In cold areas, protect plants with a loose mulch in winter, removing it in spring. Zones 5–10.

Kniphofia uvaria (Jack Hobbs)

Plant in spring or fall, 2–3 ft. (60–90 cm) apart.

Use in the perennial border or in arrangements, but they last much longer in the garden.

Lachenalia aloides

South Africa. Bulbs rarely more than 1 in. (2.5 cm) across; fleshy, white, and tunicated, producing many fibrous roots. Stems to 10 in. (25 cm). Leaves two, broadly lance-shaped, dark green with purple spots. Flowers pendent, 10–20 per spike, inner segments green tipped with burgundy, outer segments deep rose or crimson tipped with yellow. Flowers have three zones of color, which accounts for the plant often being incorrectly listed in catalogs as *L. tricolor*. Fruit a three-celled capsule with many shiny black seeds.

Blooms early spring.

Well-drained, humus-rich soil, in some sun but sheltered from the hottest rays (full sun is better in cool coastal climates), plenty of moisture when growing, less when the leaves start to turn yellow, none when leaves are withered. Zones 9–10.

Plant 2 in. (5 cm) deep, 1–2 in. (2.5–5 cm) apart.

Use for long-lasting flowers in shallow containers; plant bulbs close together. The flowers often last six to eight weeks, each bulb producing up to four spikes. Can be used outdoors in frost-free areas. Best when planted toward the front of a border. Excellent for the cool greenhouse.

Var. *aurea*, bright golden-orange.

'Nelsonii', unspotted leaves, flowers not as bright orange as var. *aurea*, tinged green.

'Pearsonii', bright orange edged with claret red.

Var. *quadricolor*, red base, then a zone of greenish yellow, outer segments tipped green, inner reddish purple.

LAPEIROUSIA
Small red iris

A genus of about 40 species from South Africa to the Arabian peninsula. The corms are woody and have a flat base. The leaves are *Iris*-like but often form a cup circling the flowering stem at the base and clothing it. The perianth tube is straight, about 2 in. (5 cm) long, with lobes opening into dainty, flat-faced flowers, usually five or six per stem. The

Lachenalia aloides (Jack Hobbs)

Lachenalia aloides var. *aurea* (Jack Hobbs)

flowers often seem to arise from the axils of the leaves because the flower stalk is so short, though it often branches; it is seldom over 6 in. (15 cm) tall.

Blooms in spring or summer, depending on the species.

Sandy, well-drained soil, in sun, moisture as needed when growing but on the dry side, withhold water when the leaves begin to turn brown. Zone 9.

Plant spring-flowering species in late summer or early fall, summer-flowering species in spring, 3–4 in. (7.5–10 cm) deep, 4–6 in. (10–15 cm) apart.

Use in the rock garden or the front of a sunny border with excellent drainage. They look good with a background of rocks and appreciate the reflected heat.

Lapeirousia corymbosa. Stems branched, to 6 in. (15 cm). Leaves usually four, lowest one curving strongly away from stem. Flowers blue or yellow, with a white star outlined in blue in center; perianth tube barely over 1 in. (2.5 cm) long; late spring to summer.

Lapeirousia silenoides. Stems 4–6 in. (10–15 cm) or less, often branched from base. Solitary basal leaf to 5 in. (12.5 cm) long; pale green bracts on stem broader and much shorter. Flowers upright, to seven per stem, with slender, cream perianth tubes to 2 in. (5 cm) long; lobes magenta to cherry red with cream and dark red markings on base, often a darker blotch on three lower segments; spring.

Leucocoryne ixioides

Chile. Bulbs small, egg-shaped, to 2 in. (5 cm) across, covered by a brown tunic. Stems 10–20 in. (25–50 cm). Leaves narrow, grasslike, to 12 in. (30 cm). Flowers large, loosely held on long pedicels in an umbel, seldom more than 12 per stem; distinguished by three short, fertile stamens and three long, sterile stamens; tepals fused into a narrow tube; lobes separate above the mouth of the tube and flare widely. Flowers white to pale blue-purple, very fragrant, sterile stamens white.

Blooms late spring to early summer.

Lapeirousia silenoides (Robert Ornduff)

Leucocoryne ixioides (International Flower Bulb Center)

Well-drained soil, in full sun, barely moist until leaves appear, then increase water. Give weak feedings of organic fertilizer in early spring if the soil is poor. Zones 9–10.

Plant in fall, 3–4 in. (7.5–10 cm) deep.

Use for long-lasting cut flowers. At 25°F (–4°C) they benefit from the protection of a mulch or a south-facing wall. They do well in bulb frames.

LEUCOJUM
Loddon lily, snowflake

A genus of about nine species from central Europe and the Mediterranean region. Closely related to *Galanthus* and similar in appearance; the easiest way to distinguish between the two is to remember that *Leucojum* (which begins with an "L") has perianth segments of equal length, so the petals are "level." In *Galanthus*, the inner and outer perianth segments are unequal. The flowers, up to five per stem, are pendent on slender pedicels; they are bell-shaped, and the tips of the tepals are often green or yellow-green. The leaves are basal, from narrow to ½ in. (12 mm) wide.

Blooms mid to late spring or early to mid autumn, depending on the species.

Leucojum aestivum

Leucojum aestivum 'Gravetye Giant'

Leucojum aestivum, detail (Jack Hobbs)

Average garden soil, in full sun except in the hottest climates, plenty of moisture in fall and spring. Zone 7.

Plant in fall, 1–2 in. (2.5–5 cm) deep.

Use in a woodland setting with filtered sunlight or at the front of the border. *Leucojum vernum* naturalizes well in grass, if adequately moist.

Leucojum aestivum. Summer snowflake. Europe, western Asia to Iran. Bulb large, egg-shaped, with a brown tunic. Stems to 20 in. (50 cm). Leaves linear, ¾ in. (2 cm) wide, with blunt keel. Flowers 1 in. (2.5 cm) across or a little larger, bell-shaped, white with green marking at tip of each tepal; usually five or six per stem, seldom more than eight, spring. **'Gravetye Giant'**, robust, free-flowering.

Leucojum vernum. Spring snowflake. Central Europe. Bulb elongated, fleshy, with thin, brown tunic. Stems 6–12 in. (15–30 cm). Leaves to 10 in. (25 cm) long, ¾ in. (2 cm) wide, shiny, green. Flowers slightly fragrant, white with green markings on tips of tepals, usually solitary, seldom more than two per stem; late winter or early spring. Naturalizes easily and should be left undisturbed. **Var.** *carpathicum*, yellow or yellow-green tips. **Var.** *vagneri*, more robust, often with two flowers per stem.

LILIUM
Lily

A genus of 100 or more species distributed throughout the temperate regions of the Northern Hemisphere. Deservedly called the aristocrats of the plant world. Hybrids are divided into various groups based on flower form. For example, trumpet lilies have long tubes, turk's caps have free tepals that strongly curve back. The true bulbs have fleshy scales which overlap loosely or tightly. The flowering stems are erect, and the leaves are arranged on the stem either scattered or in one or more whorls. The flowers of most lilies are large, and many are fragrant. They are borne in a raceme (in a few species, in an umbel) on pedicels, usually long, and can be either upright-facing, outward-facing, or pendent. The six tepals (perianth segments) may be free or joined to form a tube or trumpet. Each tepal has a nectary gland at the base. The six stamens generally have slender filaments tapering from the base, and the style is usually quite long, often protruding from the mouth of trumpet-shaped flowers. The ovary is three-celled and contains many flat, winged seeds.

Very well-drained, humus-rich soil, worked to at least 12 in. (30 cm) deep. Lilies like their feet in the shade and their heads in the sun. Give moisture when growing. Feed with a 10–10–10 fertilizer as soon as plants appear above ground in spring; repeat in six to eight weeks. Stake plants as needed.

Plant in fall or spring, at a depth that corresponds to twice the height of the bulb, 10–24 in. (25–60 cm) apart depending on the species.

Use in gardens, in containers, and as cut flowers. In the garden, lilies can be placed among shrubs to prolong the interest of a border. They

Lilium auratum var. *platyphyllum* (Eddie McRae)

complement the perennial border, and some are well adapted to the margin of the woodland.

Lilium auratum. Gold band lily. Japan. The band of gold may be very narrow or very wide; sometimes the band is red, and these forms are commonly mistaken for hybrids. Stems usually 3–7 ft. (90–210 cm), over 10 ft. (3 m) under ideal conditions, with up to 25 flowers. Leaves broad, often more than 2 in. (5 cm) wide, and to 8 in. (20 cm) long. Flowers 8–10 in. (20–25 cm) across, downward- and outward-facing on strong pedicels, bowl-shaped; tips of the tepals recurve; tepals spotted crimson or brown. At the base of the tepals are contrastingly colored stubby attachments protruding from the surface; in the center is a channel, often darker, which leads to the nectaries. *Lilium auratum* is perhaps the loveliest lily of the genus, with great form and texture, wonderful fragrance, vigorous and easy. It passes many of its fine traits on to its progeny and is a parent of many hybrids. Zone 6. **Var.** *platyphyllum* is taller and more vigorous. **Red Band Group** has a well-defined bright crimson median band.

Lilium auratum Red Band Group

Lilium canadense

Lilium canadense. Meadow lily. Canada, United States. Bulb oval, producing 1–2 in. (2.5–5 cm) long stolons with new bulbs at ends. Stems to 6 ft. (1.8 m). Leaves to 6 in. (15 cm) long and 2 in. (5 cm) wide, arranged in whorls; upper part of stem often has a few scattered leaves. Flowers to 20 per stem, bell-shaped, pendent, 3–4 in. (7.5–10 cm) across; tepals reflexed midway, lemon yellow with dark purple spots; pedicels horizontal. Prefers light shade; found in the wild on woodland fringes. Zone 5.

Lilium candidum. Madonna lily. Eastern Mediterranean region. Bulb white or yellowish, growing near surface. Basal leaves emerge in summer and persist through winter, mature 9–10 in. (22.5–25 cm) long and to 2 in. (5 cm) wide; also a few scattered leaves on the flower stalk. Stems 2–5 ft. (60–150 cm). Flowers to 20 per stem, held close to stem on sturdy pedicels, pure white, to 5 in. (12.5 cm) across, sweetly fragrant; tepals flare about midway and overlap at base;

early summer. Unlike other lilies, bulbs should be planted shallowly, only ½–1 in. (12–25 mm) deep, in late summer. Foliage should not remain wet in spring. Zone 6. **'Aureo-marginatum'**, leaves with prominent yellow margin. **'Plenum'**, double-flowered, tall. **'Purpureum'**, flowers and bulbs streaked purplish red. **'Variegatum'**, leaves with yellowish-white blotches.

Lilium chalcedonicum. Red martagon, scarlet turk's cap lily. Bulb yellowish, fairly large, egg-shaped, about 3 in. (7.5 cm) across and length. Stems to 4 ft. (1.2 m). Leaves scattered, numerous; lower leaves horizontal, upper leaves held close to stem. Flowers to 10 per stem, turk's-cap form, brilliant red, sometimes spotted, glistening as if lacquered; early summer. Prefers warm, somewhat alkaline soil and should be left undisturbed. Zone 5. **Var. *maculatum***, scarlet flowers spotted black.

Lilium formosanum. Taiwan. Bulb nearly globe-shaped, 1½ in. (4 cm) across. Leaves

Lilium candidum 'Cascade Strain' (Eddie McRae)

Lilium formosanum (Jack Hobbs)

Lilium formosanum (Jack Hobbs)

glossy, to 8 in. (20 cm) long, narrow, ½ in. (12 mm) or less wide, densely clothing entire stem. Flowers trumpet-shaped, very fragrant, white, pendent. Populations at lower elevations are up to 6 ft. (1.8 m) tall and produce up to eight flowers per stem, pure white, to 10 in. (25 cm) long; late summer. Zones 5–11. Plants from the highest populations, known as var. *pricei*, are only 1–2 ft. (30–60 cm) tall and have flowers to 5 in. (12.5 cm) long, tepals with red reverse and rich red keel; mid summer. Intermediate forms occur between these extremes. No form is long-lived.

Lilium japonicum. Bamboo lily. Japan. Stems 24–30 in. (60–75 cm), rarely more; stem-rooting. Leaves sparse, scattered. Flowers shell pink, funnel-shaped, up to five flowers per stem, 3–4 in. (7.5–10 cm) across; tepals to 6 in. (15 cm) long. Requires a cool root-run and good drainage. Zones 5–11.

Lilium lancifolium (syn. *L. tigrinum*). Tiger lily, devil lily. Stems to 60 in., blackish, coated with light gray or white hairs like cobwebs; stem-rooting. Shiny dark purple bulbils produced in leaf axils, often three per axil. Flowers bright orange, sometimes with pinkish tinge, heavily spotted dark purple, to 4 in. (10 cm) in diameter, pendent; tepals strongly reflexed. Strong, horizontal pedicels often carry secondary flowers. '**Flore Pleno**', double.

Lilium longiflorum. Easter lily. Japan. Bulb round, white or yellowish, 2½ in. (6.5 cm) long; many commercial forms are larger. Stems to 3 ft. (90 cm), shorter when forced. Leaves shiny green, to 7 in. (17.5 cm) long and almost 1 in. (2.5 cm) wide. Flowers up to nine per stem, very fragrant, pure white, outward-facing, funnel-shaped; tepals 5–7 in. (12.5–17.5 cm) long, slightly curling back at tips; late summer. Plants in flower for Easter are forced. Zones 5–11. '**Albo-marginatum**', bluish-green leaves with white margins.

Lilium martagon. Martagon lily, turk's-cap lily. Eurasia. Bulb egg-shaped, scales yellow. Stems sturdy, to 6 ft. (1.8 m). Leaves arranged in whorls but occasionally scattered, 6 in. (15 cm) long and 2 in. (5 cm) or more wide. Flowers to 50 per stem,

Lilium lancifolium

Lilium regale

Lilium 'Adelina', Asiatic hybrid
(Eddie McRae)

Lilium 'Beatrix', Asiatic hybrid
(Jack Hobbs)

Lilium 'La Toya', Asiatic hybrid (Jack Hobbs)

pendent; tepals reflexed midway, pale to deep dull pink, variably spotted brownish violet, 1½ in. (4 cm) long, thick, with a distinct raised keel on reverse; stamens prominent. Easy to grow in good soil in light shade; useful in light woodland, borders, and among shrubs. Zones 4–9.

Lilium philadelphicum. Wood lily. United States. Bulbs produce short stolons, with new bulbs produced alongside old ones. Stems 3–4 ft. (90–120 cm). Leaves held horizontally in whorls, to 4 in. (10 cm) long, ½ in. (12 mm) wide. Flowers in an umbel of two to five, cup-shaped, orange to deep red with deep maroon spots, upright-facing; tepals distinctively narrowed at base; early to mid summer depending on elevation and latitude. Zones 4–10. **Var. *andinum***, pale yellow to deep purple-red flowers.

Lilium pumilum. Coral lily. North Korea, Manchuria, Mongolia. Stems wiry, 24–30 in. (60–75 cm). Leaves very narrow, clustered in middle of stem with a few leaves above and below. Flowers pendent, brilliant red, sometimes sparsely spotted black, just over 1 in. (2.5 cm) across, flattened turk's-cap form, to 20 per stem;

Lilium 'Orange Pixie', Asiatic hybrid (Jack Hobbs)

Lilium 'Quickstep', Asiatic hybrid (Eddie McRae)

Lilium 'Star Gazer',
Oriental hybrid
(Eddie McRae)

Lilium 'Black Dragon',
Trumpet hybrid

Lilium 'Golden Splendor',
Trumpet hybrid

Lilium 'American Eagle', Oriental hybrid (Eddie McRae)

Lilium 'Jamboree', Oriental hybrid

Lilium 'Golden Temple', Trumpet hybrid (Eddie McRae)

Lilium 'Pink Perfection', Trumpet hybrid (Eddie McRae)

early summer. Zones 5–9. **'Golden Gleam'** and **'Yellow Bunting'** have yellow flowers.

    Lilium regale. Regal lily. China. Stems 4–6 ft. (1.2–1.8 m); stem-rooting, with many stem bulblets. Leaves scattered, dark green, 5 in. (12.5 cm) long, ¼ in. (6 mm) wide. Pedicels concentrated near top of stem, decreasing in length toward top to produce a pyramidal inflorescence. Flowers fragrant, to 30 per stem, trumpet-shaped, to 6 in. (15 cm) across; tepals to 6 in. (15 cm) long, flaring midway, white within, throat strong yellow, reverse rose purple along midrib. Perhaps the finest trumpet lily, still offered in catalogs, holding its own against many striking cultivars; excellent cut flower; deserves to be in every garden worthy of the name. It grows well in a wide range of soils, but drainage must be perfect. Zones 5–9.

    Lilium speciosum. Japanese lily. Japan, China, Taiwan. Stems to 7 ft. (2.1 m) but usually less; stem-rooting. Leaves scattered, 6–7 in. (15–17.5 cm) long and often more than 2 in. (5 cm) wide. Strong pedicels may carry secondary and even tertiary flowers. Flowers pendent, sweetly fragrant, to 6 in. (15 cm) across, rose to carmine with white margins, with many deep pink spots and stubby attachments protruding from the surface, and apple-green nectary channels near base; tepals wavy at margins, strongly curled back and twisted; stamens prominent, arching gracefully and circling the slightly longer style; late summer. Zones 6–9.

    Lilium ×testaceum. Nankeen lily. Garden hybrid (*L. candidum* × *L. chalcedonicum*). Stems 4–5 ft. (1.2–1.5 m). Flowers pale yellow with red spots, early summer. Still widely grown. Zone 6.

LYCORIS
Spider lily, hurricane lily

A genus of 8 to 17 species from China and Japan, resembling the related *Nerine*. Spider lily flowers are funnel-shaped and can be irregular in shape. The perianth segments are more or less curled back; stamens are very prominent when perianth segments curl back. The leaves are straplike, emerge after the flower stalks. The bulbs are not unlike large narcissus bulbs, with a short neck and membranous tunic.

Blooms late summer or early fall.

Well-drained, moisture-retentive soil, in full sun, moisture when growing but dry in early summer. Give a balanced fertilizer as the leaves emerge. Give a second application with higher phosphates and potash when leaves are full grown. Zones 7–10.

Plant in fall or late winter, 1–2 in. (2.5–5 cm) deep (so that after the soil settles, the neck will be at the surface), 8–10 in. (20–25 cm) apart.

Use in borders. Especially popular in the U.S. Southeast, where they are sometimes called hurricane lilies because their flowering coincides with the hurricane season. They add late-summer color to supplement spring- or summer-flowering perennials. If they are grown in this way, however, care must be taken to keep them dry until they start into growth; this can be facilitated by growing them in pots and plunging them in position at the right time.

Lycoris ×*albiflora*. White spider lily. Japan. Stems 18–24 in. (45–60 cm). Leaves straplike, ½ in. (12 mm) wide, with pale center line, 20–24 in. (50–60 cm) long. Flowers three to five per stem, creamy white, 2 in. (5 cm) long; tube less than half the length of tepals; tepals recurve; fall.

Lycoris incarnata. China, Japan. Stems 12–18 in. (30–45 cm). Leaves similar to those of *L. aurea* but brighter green. Flowers 10–12 per stem on short pedicels, white aging to light rose, to 3 in. (7.5 cm) wide, fragrant; tube short; lobes not reflexed or wavy; late summer.

Lycoris radiata. Spider lily, red spider lily. China, Japan. Stems to 18 in. (45 cm). Leaves narrow, strap-shaped, green with lighter median stripe, 18–20 in. (45–60 cm) long. Flowers four to six per stem, pink to deep red or scarlet, nodding, irregular; lobes much reflexed and wavy on margins; late summer.

Lycoris squamigera. Magic lily, resurrection lily. China, Japan, Korea. Stems to 2 ft. (60 cm). Leaves five or six, produced in spring, 12 in. (30 cm) long, 1 in. (2.5 cm) wide. Flowers large, bluish pink, late summer. The hardiest species.

Lycoris radiata (Harry B. Hay)

Moraea tricolor

South Africa. Root a fibrous-coated corm. Stems to 6 in. (15 cm). Leaves erect, usually three sheathing base of stem. Flowers yellow, pink, rarely red, or light purple; yellow nectar guides often edged with crimson. A delightful little species.

Blooms winter to early spring.

Tolerates a wide range of soils, in sun, moist when growing, dry otherwise. Apply a general fertilizer after leaves emerge. Zone 9.

Plant in fall, 2 in. (5 cm) deep, several inches apart.

Moraea tricolor (Robert Ornduff)

Use in frost-free areas. Attractive in shallow containers. A good cut flower. Although the brilliant flowers with their eyelike markings often last only a day, they are numerous per stem and thus present an outstanding, ongoing display.

MUSCARI
Grape hyacinth

A genus of 30 or more species from the Mediterranean and West Asia. The bulb is globe-shaped and fleshy, sometimes with a thin tunic. The leaves are narrow and linear, generally one to four per bulb, and basal. They often appear in fall, followed by the flowers in spring, and continue to grow after flowering, withering into dormancy for only two or three months in summer. The flowers are carried on a leafless stem in crowded racemes. The small perianth is composed of six fused lobes, which may be constricted at the mouth. In many species, the florets at the top of the stem are different from those below, perhaps as a device to attract pollinators; the difference may be one of color (dark vs. light), of form, or of both.

Blooms spring.

Average garden soil, in sun or dappled shade, dry in summer. The fall-growing foliage may be damaged below about 15°F (–9°C).

Plant in fall, 2–3 in. (5–7.5 cm) deep, 4–5 in. (10–12.5 cm) apart.

Use in masses to make an impact. They add the blue that is often lacking in spring borders to complement other spring-flowering bulbs. Plant them among shrubs and trees where they can remain undisturbed; once established, no amount of disturbance is likely to eradicate them. They are also very effective massed in containers, even hanging baskets. Some are excellent, fragrant cut flowers. All are very easy to grow.

Muscari armeniacum. Balkans to Caucasus. Stems 6–8 in. (15–20 cm). Leaves to 12 in. (30 cm) long, narrow, channeled, four to eight per bulb. Flowers in long racemes, deep purple-blue with white rim, fragrant, mid spring. Commonly grown, rapid increaser; excellent cut flower. Zones 6–9. **'Blue Spike'**, long-lasting, soft blue double. **'Early Giant'**, large, deep purple-blue.

Muscari aucheri. Turkey. Stems 2–8 in. (5–20 cm). Flowers indigo blue with white rim, late spring. Zones 6–9.

Muscari azureum. Turkey, Caucasus. Stems 4–6 in. (10–15 cm). Leaves short at flowering, later 10–12 in. (25–30 cm) long, gray-green. Flowers bright blue with narrow, dark blue median stripe, in compact raceme; early spring. Very hardy; likes well-drained soil and tolerates full sun or light shade, thus ideal for planting in drifts in shrub borders. Zones 6–9. **'Album'**, white. **'Amphibolis'**, light blue, slightly larger flowers.

Muscari armeniacum 'Blue Spike'

Muscari armeniacum 'Early Giant'

Muscari botryoides (foreground) with *Pulsatilla* (background) (Jack Hobbs)

Muscari latifolium

Muscari botryoides. France, Italy. Stems 4–10 in. (10–25 cm). Leaves two to four, narrow, stiff. Flowers small, closely held, sky blue with white rim, mid to late spring. Zones 6–9. **'Album'**, white, more common in gardens than the type.

Muscari comosum. Tassel hyacinth. Mediterranean region. Bulb pinkish. Stems 8–12 in. (20–30 cm). Upper flowers purple, sterile, ribbonlike; lower flowers greenish brown, fertile; mid to late spring. Zones 4–9. **'Epirus Giant'**, 24–30 in. (60–75 cm) tall, raceme 20 in. (50 cm). **'Plumosum'** (feather hyacinth) has all sterile flowers, mauve.

Muscari latifolium. Turkey. Stems 6–12 in. (15–30 cm). Leaf solitary, lance-shaped, narrow at base, erect, tends to overshadow the flowers. Fertile lower flowers violet, sterile upper flowers bright blue; late spring. Zones 6–9.

Muscari macrocarpum. Greece, Turkey. Stems to 10 in. (25 cm), often leaning. Flowers yellow with brownish rims, very fragrant, mid spring. Zones 6–9.

Muscari neglectum. North Africa, Europe, Asia. Stems to 6 in. (15 cm). Leaves narrow, to 12 in. (30 cm) long. Upper flowers midblue, sterile; lower flowers fertile, deep blue, almost black, with white rim at mouth; early spring. Very easy to grow, spreads rapidly. Zones 4–9.

NARCISSUS
Daffodil

A genus of 50 to 70 species from Europe, North Africa, and the Near East; naturalized in many parts of Europe. Narcissus bulbs range from ¼ in. (6 mm) to more than 4 in. (10 cm) across, some with a distinct neck, others with a reduced neck. All have brown tunics. The stems are always unbranched, more or less flattened, and leafless. The flowers, either solitary or borne in an umbel, are white or pale to deep yellow, sometimes bicolored. The position of the flowers is usually slightly pendent but ranges from fully upright to quite drooping.

The distinctive form of the daffodil flower arises from its having two prominent structures. The six perianth segments or tepals—three outer, slightly larger ones and three inner ones—are fused at the base into a tube and then separate and spread to form the corolla, the wide, flat part of the flower. At the mouth of the tube raised structures, normally fused, extend from the upper surface of the tepals to form the corona, also called the "trumpet" or "cup" depending on its proportions. The corolla and corona may be the same color, or contrasting colors. Sometimes the corona has zones of red or green, and these have been exploited by hybridizers in the quest for new color forms. The six stamens and the style with its three-lobed stigma extend from the tube but usually not beyond the rim of the corona.

Blooms in spring.

Well-drained soil, in full sun, moisture when growing, dry in summer. Allow leaves to die down completely. Never remove green foliage. Braiding or bundling the leaves is harmful. If you can't stand the way they look after flowering, gather the leaves in your hand and smooth them neatly to one side; at this point they are lax enough to lie where you put them, but they are still manufacturing food and supporting growth. Hardiness varies by species, Zones 5–10 for hybrids.

Plant in fall, 5–6 in. (12.5–15 cm) deep, 4 in. (10 cm) apart.

Use almost anywhere. In the woodland they can be naturalized; in the garden they can be planted with spring-flowering annuals; in shrub borders and other permanent plantings they add spring color. They make excellent cut flowers. The smaller species are ideal for the rock garden and sunny corners of annual and perennial borders. The careful selection of early, mid season, and late-flowering types can produce a very long flowering period. In warm Mediterranean climates, the most persistent flowering is obtained from the Tazetta and Hoop Petticoat Groups, which do not flourish where winter temperatures often drop below about 25°F (–4°C). The trumpet and large-cupped daffodils do best in regions with a decidedly chill winter and may dwindle where they do not experience this; however, they can still be grown in warm regions as bedding plants for one season and then discarded.

Narcissus bulbocodium

Narcissus jonquilla

Narcissus bulbocodium. Hoop petticoat daffodil. Spain, Portugal, France, North Africa. Stems 4–10 in. (10–25 cm). Leaves dark green, to 20 in. (50 cm) long but usually much less, very narrow, two to four per bulb. Corolla much reduced; corona very large, varying in shape: globular, narrowly goblet-shaped, wide open and flaring, or nearly trumpet-shaped. Flowers usually solitary but up to eight per stem, pale to deep yellow, often flushed green on reverse of corolla segments; early to mid spring. Zones 6–10. **Subsp.** *bulbocodium*, leaves more or less erect, tube and perianth tinged green, corona regularly obconical, not narrowed at the rim; **var.** *citrinus* has pale lemon-yellow flowers, stems to 6 in; **var.** *conspicuus* has deep yellow flowers, stems 4–6 in. (10–15 cm).

Narcissus cyclamineus. Portugal, Spain. Stems 4–8 in. (10–20 cm). Leaves bright green, 6–10 in. (15–25 cm) long, ¼ in. (6 mm) wide. Flowers rich, bright yellow, solitary on sharply downcurved pedicels; corona to ¾ in. (2 cm) long, narrowly tubular, margin slightly expanded and frilly. Corolla segments ¾ in. (2 cm) long, completely folded curve back to cover the pedicel—as E. A. Bowles wrote in 1955, "like the laid back ears of a kicking horse." Early spring. Good for the damp places in the garden. Zones 6–9.

Narcissus jonquilla. Jonquil. Spain, Portugal. Bulbs small, dark brown. Stems to 12 in. (30 cm). Leaves dark green, rushlike, to 12 in. (30 cm) or more. Flowers rich golden yellow, in umbels of up to six, to 2 in. (5 cm) in diameter. Corolla segments to ¾ in. (2 cm) long; corona shallowly cup-shaped, seldom over ¼ in. (6 mm) long, often over ½ in. (12 mm) in diameter. Flowering mid spring. Long grown for its fragrance. **'Dickcissel'**, bright yellow flowers. **'Flore Pleno'** (syn. 'Plenus'), a double form known as Queen Anne's double jonquil. **Var.** *henriquesii* has one or two flowers on 2-in. (5-cm) pedicels held horizontally, segments spreading and not overlapping, margins incurved.

Narcissus minor. Pyrenees, Spain. Stems 6–7 in. (15–17.5 cm). Leaves to 8 in. (20 cm) long, ¼ in. (6 mm) wide. Flowers solitary, pendent or hor-

Narcissus jonquilla 'Dickcissel'

izontal; corolla segments to 1 in. (2.5 cm) long, sometimes twisted, pale to deep yellow; corona almost 1 in. (2.5 cm) long, deep yellow, slightly flared at mouth, with lobed or dentate rim; early spring. Zones 4–9. **'Cedric Morris'**, pale yellow.

Narcissus ×*odorus*. Campernelle jonquil. Garden hybrid (*N. pseudonarcissus* × *N. jonquilla*). Stems to 16 in. (40 cm). Leaves to 20 in. (50 cm) long, strongly V-shaped in cross section, bright green. Flowers one to four, fragrant, bright yellow; corolla segments just over 1 in. (2.5 cm) long and ½ in. (12 mm) wide; corona to 1 in. (2.5 cm) long, wider than long, lobed on margin. Zones 6–9.

Narcissus poeticus in the wild

Narcissus triandrus (Jack Hobbs)

Narcissus 'King Alfred', Trumpet hybrid (Jack Hobbs)

Narcissus 'Accent', Large cupped hybrid

Narcissus poeticus. Poet's narcissus, pheasant's eye narcissus. France, Spain, Italy, Greece. Stems 8–16 in. (20–40 cm). Leaves 8–16 in. (20–40 cm) long, to ¼ in. (6 mm) wide, usually four per bulb, flat. Flowers fragrant, usually solitary. Perianth segments ¾–1½ in. (2–4 cm) long, white or pale cream; corona ½–1 in. (12–25 mm) long, disc-shaped to cylindrical, yellow with red rim; late spring, about the latest daffodil in the garden. Zones 4–9. **Subsp. poeticus**, leaves to ½ in. (12 mm) wide, perianth segments about 1 in. (2.5 cm) long, without a distinct claw at the tip; corona more or less discoid, to ¾ in. (2 cm) across, anthers held at two different levels. Has two varieties: **var. physaloides**, spathes inflated in bud stage, flowers pure white, corona small, greenish yellow with crimson rim; **var. recurvus**, corolla segments recurving, corona with green center and red rim above yellow cup.

Narcissus triandrus. Angel's tears. Spain, Portugal, and NW France. Stems to 10 in. (25 cm), usually less. Leaves narrow, dark green, 6–12 in. (15–30 cm) long. Flowers pendent, white, cream, or clear yellow. Corolla segments ¼–¾ in. (6–20 mm) long, strongly reflexed; corona cup-shaped, as wide as deep, ¼–½ in. (6–12 mm) long. Flowering mid spring. Zones 4–9. 'Albus', common in cultivation, is a color variant that occurs in many wild populations.

Narcissus hybrids are divided into several groups, several of which are illustrated here. **Trumpet Group**: one flower per stem, with a trumpet or corona as long or longer than the perianth segments. **Large-cupped Group**: one flower per stem, the cup or corona more than a third, but less than equal to, the length of the perianth segments. **Double Group**: flowers double. **Triandrus Group**: mostly short-stemmed, multiflowered, with reflexed corolla. **Cyclamineus Group**: plants medium-sized, early-flowering with more or less strongly reflexed corolla. **Tazetta Group**: several small, fragrant flowers per stem. **Papillon Group**: coronas split, corona segments usually in a single whorl of six and alternate to the perianth segments.

Narcissus 'Erlicheer', Double hybrid (Jack Hobbs)

Narcissus 'Hawera',
Triandrus hybrid

Narcissus 'Garden Princess',
Cyclamineus hybrid
(Jack Hobbs)

Narcissus 'March
Sunshine', Cyclamineus
hybrid (Jack Hobbs)

Narcissus 'Avalanche', Tazetta hybrid (Jack Hobbs)

Narcissus 'Tète á Tète', Cyclamineus hybrid (Jack Hobbs)

Narcissus 'Soleil d'Or', Tazetta hybrid (Jack Hobbs)

Narcissus 'White Owl', Tazetta hybrid (Jack Hobbs)

Narcissus 'Dolly Mollinger', Papillon hybrid (Jack Hobbs)

Nectaroscordum siculum subsp. *bulgaricum*, buds (International Flower Bulb Center)

Nectaroscordum siculum subsp. *bulgaricum*, flowers (International Flower Bulb Center)

Nectaroscordum siculum
Sicilian honey garlic

Eastern Mediterranean region. Bulb white, egg-shaped, to 1 in. (2.5 cm) across. Stems to 30 in. (75 cm). Leaves ¾ in. (2 cm) wide, to 15 in. (37.5 cm) long, basal, V-shaped in cross section. Flowers bell-shaped, ½ in. (12 mm) long, to 30 per umbel, green with purple and white margins, sometimes reddish. Plants have a typical onion smell when crushed. Easy to grow.

Blooms early to mid summer.

Any well-drained soil, in full sun, moderate moisture when growing. Zones 5–9.

Plant bulbs 2 in. (5 cm) deep, 10 in. (25 cm) apart.

Use in groups in the sunny border, where their subtle colors are effective among gray foliage. They can become invasive by self-sowing, so the flower-heads should be removed before the seed ripens.

Subsp. *bulgaricum*, the form usually seen in gardens, flowers white or cream, flushed gray-green at base, rose pink within.

NERINE
Spider lily

A genus of about 25 species from southern Africa, closely related to *Amaryllis* and *Lycoris*. The bulb is tunicated. The inflorescence is an umbel of two or more flowers with six narrow petals each, joined at the base. The flowers are borne on individual pedicels, carried erect or horizontally, seldom pendent, with one or two tepals curving more than the others. The stamens, often curved, extend well beyond the perianth. The leaves are threadlike, linear, or strap-shaped, appearing with or after flowering.

Blooms in fall.

Well-drained, reasonably rich garden soil, in full sun, moisture when growing, none when leaves start to yellow.

Plant in spring, with their necks at soil level in containers, but with 3 in. (7.5 cm) of soil over them outdoors in mild climates, deeper where frost may occur, 10–12 in. (25–30 cm) apart.

Use anywhere unusual-looking flowers in bright colors are wanted. Good among shrubs to

Nerine bowdenii 'E. B. Anderson' (Harry B. Hay)

extend the flowering season into late summer and fall. In the mixed border they are best planted in bold groups. The smaller-growing species are excellent container plants.

Nerine bowdenii. South Africa. Stems to 2 ft. (60 cm). Leaves glossy, dark green, emerging before flowering and dying back in the winter. Flowers 10–15 in a loose umbel, carmine pink with darker median band; tepals 2–3 in. (5–7.5 cm) long, with wavy edges and tips curled back. Can withstand a little frost. One of the most striking nerines, but its popularity in gardens may be due as much to its hardiness as to its colorful flowers. Flowers open very wide; this characteristic and its hardiness have resulted in its being much used in hybridizing. Zones 8–11. **'Alba'**, white with a hint of pink. **'E. B. Anderson'**, true pink. **'Pink Triumph'**, salmon pink. **'Wellsii'**, solitary flower.

Nerine sarniensis. Guernsey lily. South Africa. Stems stout, to 24 in. (60 cm). Leaves three to five, strap-shaped, about 12 in. (30 cm) long, produced after flowering and persisting

Nerine bowdenii

Nerine sarniensis 'Fothergillii Major' (Jack Hobbs)

through winter, withering in spring. Flowers to 20 per umbel, upward-facing, white to rose and deep carmine; surface iridescent, highly reflective; stamens and anthers prominent, golden yellow. Zones 8–10. **'Bettina'**, rose pink with darker vein. **'Blush Beauty'**, stems to 40 in. (100 cm), flowers pale pink. **'Fothergillii Major'**, dazzling vermilion-scarlet, large umbels. **'Guy Fawkes'**, light cerise.

ORNITHOGALUM
Chincherinchee

A genus of about 120 species from the temperate regions of Europe, Asia, and Africa. Many species are hardy. The rootstock is a globe-shaped bulb with a white or brown tunic. A few species have orange-red-yellow flowers, while most are white with a green median stripe on each tepal. The flowers are borne in a corymb or raceme; in some species, the inflorescence appears at ground level amid a rosette of leaves. The tepals are of similar size and shape, free to the base and spreading widely to produce starry flowers. The filaments are flat, almost petal-like in some species. The leaves are basal and linear, often past their peak when the flower spike matures.

Well-drained, sandy loam, adequate moisture when leaves are growing.

Plant 2–3 in. (5–7.5 cm) deep, 4–12 in. (10–30 cm) apart, depending on the spcies.

Use in bold groups in the garden. The hardy species can be naturalized in grass. Some species are especially good for planting among shrub borders in mild climates. The dwarf species are good container plants and interesting in rock gardens. *Ornithogalum thyrsoides* is grown in quantity for cut flowers.

Ornithogalum arabicum. Mediterranean region. Stems 20–30 in. (50–75 cm). Leaves to 1 in. (2.5 cm) wide, 15 in. (37.5 cm) long. Flowers

Ornithogalum dubium

Ornithogalum arabicum (International Flower Bulb Center)

often over 2 in. (5 cm) in diameter, pure white with distinctive black ovary; flowers lower on stem have longer pedicels, resulting in a flattened inflorescence. Zones 8–10.

Ornithogalum dubium. Yellow chincherinchee. South Africa. Stems 8–12 in. (20–30 cm). Leaves short, broad, in a basal rosette. Flowers to 25 per stem, golden yellow to deep orange, sometimes white, with near-black central zone; lower pedicels longer than upper, resulting in a flat raceme; early to mid spring. Requires a dry dormancy in late summer. Best grown frost-free. Zones 8–10.

Ornithogalum nutans. Silver bells. Europe. Stems and leaves 12–18 in. (30–45 cm). Flowers 3–12 per stem, white with green midrib on reverse; pedicels short; raceme often somewhat one-sided. Flowering late spring through early summer. Prefers shade and will naturalize in woodland. Zones 7–10.

Ornithogalum oligophyllum. Balkan Peninsula, Turkey. Stems to 6 in. (15 cm). Leaves few, short, about 1/2 in. (12 mm) wide. Flowers to five per stem, about 1 in. (2.5 cm) across, white with green reverse, early spring. Zones 6–9.

Ornithogalum thyrsoides. Chincherinchee, wonder flower. South Africa. Bulb relatively large, greenish. Stems to 2 ft. (60 cm) but often much shorter. Flowers pure white sometimes with dark center; prominent yellow stamens; many cup-shaped flowers densely carried on short raceme, or more widely spaced on taller stems. Plant in spring to flower in late summer, lift, and overwinter dry. In mild climates, bulbs left in the ground multiply quickly. Appreciates summer moisture but needs free-draining soil. The onomatopoetic common name (originally rendered "tinkerinteés") imitates the sound produced when the stems are rubbed together. Flower stalk, leaves, and flowers are toxic to grazing animals. Zones 9–11.

Ornithogalum nutans

Ornithogalum thyrsoides (Jack Hobbs)

Ornithogalum thyrsoides, detail

Ornithogalum umbellatum

Oxalis adenophylla (International Flower Bulb Center)

Ornithogalum umbellatum. Star of Bethlehem. Europe, Turkey, North Africa. Stems 6–8 in. (15–20 cm). Leaves six to nine, 6–12 in. (15–30 cm) long. Flowers 6–20 per stem, white, with green stripes on reverse, almost unnoticeable flowers are wide open. Flowers open late in the day and close at night; late spring. A good plant for the wild garden but can be quite invasive through self-sowing. Zones 5–10.

OXALIS
Sorrel

A genus of 500 to 800 species. A few of these are from the northern and southern temperate zones, but the majority are found in South Africa and tropical and subtropical South America. Most of the species are not bulbous, and many of them are invasive plants that can become pests in the garden, seeding rapidly and difficult to erad-

Oxalis lutea

icate. A number are charming, more or less well-behaved species in commerce. Most species are low-growing. The deciduous leaves resemble clover, with three or sometimes more leaflets. They often droop and fold up at night or on very hot days. Flower colors include yellow, pink, orange, red, white, and lavender. The flowers open only in the sunshine. They have five overlapping sepals which are twisted spirally in bud. The open flower is broadly funnel-shaped to flat, with a cup in the center. There are 10 stamens in two series of five each.

Well-drained soil, never clay, in full sun (except for woodland species), moisture at all times but can survive dry conditions in summer. Hardiness varies by species. Some species do not flourish where temperatures drop below 25°F (–4°C); others are fairly cold-tolerant but should not be wet in winter.

Plant 1 in. (2.5 cm) deep, 3–4 in. (7.5–10 cm) apart.

Use in masses at the front of a low border or in a wall. Easy to grow, they are good plants for the low-maintenance garden, but most go dormant for part of the year and cannot be relied on for foliage effect year-round. Except for the high-alpine species, any oxalis introduced to the garden should be treated as a potential invader and tried initially in some confined space, such as a hanging basket, window box, or other container set over pavement. The seeds are dispersed explosively and can spread rapidly over a large area.

Oxalis adenophylla. Chile, Argentina. Often marketed as "pink buttercups," though not related to buttercups (*Ranunculus*). Tubers small, elongated, covered with a mass of fibers made up of bases of old leaves. Stems 2–4 in. (5–10 cm). Leaves in compact rosettes, glaucous, with many leaflets. Flowers 1 in. (2.5 cm) across, one per stalk, pale to deep lilac pink, paler near base, dark purple center spots at base; late spring to early summer. Zones 5–9.

Oxalis purpurea

Oxalis purpurea 'Alba' (Jack Hobbs)

Oxalis regnellii (W. George Schmid)

Pancratium maritimum (Maurice Boussard)

Oxalis lutea. South Africa. Bulb with gummy tunic. Stems to 2 in. (5 cm) tall. Flowers deep yellow, late fall to early spring. Zones 8–10.

Oxalis purpurea. South Africa. Bulb blackish, globe- to egg-shaped. Stems 1–2 in. (2.5–5 cm). Flowers reddish purple with yellow tube; autumn to late winter. Zones 8–10.

Oxalis regnellii. Peru, Brazil, Bolivia, Paraguay, and Argentina. Rhizome brownish, tuberculate. Stems to 10 in. (25 cm). Leaves green mottled with purple. Flowers pale pink to white.

Oxalis tetraphylla. Good luck leaf plant, lucky clover, four-leaved clover. Mexico. Bulb roundish, black or dark brown, scaly, to 1 1/2 in. (4 cm) across, edible. Stems 10–12 in. (25–30 cm). Leaves cloverlike with four red-spotted leaflets. Flowers in an umbel, lilac pink, rose, or reddish, with greenish-yellow throat; mid to late summer. Zone 8. **Var. alba**, pure white. **'Iron Cross'**, cross-shaped brown markings on leaves.

Pancratium maritimum
Sea lily, sea daffodil

Mediterranean coast. Bulb large, globe-shaped, with pale scales and very long neck, slightly poisonous. Stems to 2 ft. (60 cm). Leaves persistent but not truly evergreen, strap-shaped. Flowers borne in an umbel, shaped like a large trumpet daffodil, white with green median stripe on reverse, fragrant; corona long and toothed. Fruit a smooth, round capsule.

Blooms late summer.

Very well drained, sandy soil, full sun in all but the hottest, driest climates, where they tolerate some shade during the height of the day. Keep moist and do not allow to dry out while active growth is taking place. Water is not essential after flowering. Zones 8–10.

Plant in spring, with 2–3 in. (5–7.5 cm) of soil over the top, about 12 in. (30 cm) apart. Give weak feedings of fertilizer as soon as the leaves emerge.

Pancratium maritimum, seed (Arne Strid)

Use in milder climates, among shrubs in a sunny border to extend the period of interest, and especially in spots where the fragrance can be enjoyed. Best against a sunny wall, with a dry period in late summer

Polianthes tuberosa
Tuberose

Wild origin uncertain. Rootstock a short rhizome comprised of thickened roots with bulblike bases. Stems to 3 ft. (90 cm). Leaves basal, narrow, to 2 ft. (60 cm) long, sheathing stem. Flowers borne in pairs on terminal racemes, to 30 per stem, very fragrant, white, waxy, curved at base, opening to 2 in. (5 cm) across. Individual flowers last a long time before dropping; buds open in succession over a long period.

Blooms mid to late summer, every other year.

Good garden soil, in full sun, moist at planting time, but little water until the leaves emerge, then keep plants moist and feed with organic liquid fertilizer every two weeks. Zones 9–10.

Plant in spring when the ground is warm and night temperatures are above 55°F (13°C). Where nights remain colder later than May, start plants indoors in pots and transplant carefully to outdoor sites. Set rhizomes 3 in. (7.5 cm) deep and 8–10 in. (20–25 cm) apart. For cutflower production, set 4–6 in. (10–15 cm) apart in rows 2 ft. (60 cm) apart.

Use for cut flowers or in a summer border. Place them where the fragrance can be enjoyed. They can be planted in shrub borders in mild climates and left undisturbed for many years. They can also be grown in containers but may require support. An excellent plant for the cool greenhouse.

'**Mexican**', single flowers, worthy of garden space.

'**The Pearl**', sweetly scented double flowers, popular with florists.

Polianthes tuberosa (Jack Hobbs)

Puschkinia scilloides
Striped squill
Turkey, Caucasus, Iran, Syria, Iraq, and Lebanon. Leaves shiny, green, usually two, basal, 4–6 in. (10–15 cm) long, present at flowering. Flowers on short pedicels on a brownish, leafless stem, 4–8 in. (10–20 cm) high at maturity but usually much shorter at flowering time. There are six to eight flowers per stem, pale to mid blue, with a darker blue stripe down the center of each segment. They are about 1 in. (2.5 cm) across or slightly less; in the center is a corona formed by the filaments.

Blooms in early spring.

Rich, moisture-retentive soil, never waterlogged. Zones 4–6.

Plant 2 in. (5 cm) deep in fall, 4–6 in. (10–15 cm) apart.

Use in masses for a good early spring display. Plant in areas where it can be allowed to self-sow, which it does quite readily. Suitable for rock gardens and wild gardens in full sun or partial shade. Grows well among deciduous shrubs. A good container plant; looks best planted closely in a shallow pan.

Var. *libanotica*, the most common form in horticulture, has smaller, pale blue flowers with blunt corona lobes; its cultivar **'Alba'** has white flowers with stripes.

Ranunculus acontifolius
Europe. Roots tuberous, quite small, with "claws" on the underside. Stems 12 in. (30 cm). Leaves lobed. Flowers white. The **Tecolote®** mix from California features mostly fully double flowers 3–6 in. (7.5–15 cm) wide, in a range of colors including bicolored picotee, gold, pastel mix, pink, red, rose, salmon, sunset orange, white, and yellow. The **Hadeco** mix from South Africa is also known for its large, double flowers in a variety of colors.

Blooms spring.

Sandy soil, in full sun, moderate moisture when growing. Too much water causes yellowing of the foliage. Zones 6–9.

Plant in spring, when danger of heavy frost is past, or in fall in warmer areas, 1 in. (2.5 cm) deep, 8–10 in. (20–25 cm) apart.

Use in rock gardens in warm regions. Florist ranunculus are good cut flowers and can also be

Puschkinia scilloides (International Flower Bulb Center)

Ranunculus, Hadeco
hybrids, mixed

Ranunculus, Hadeco
hybrids, yellow

Ranunculus, Hadeco
hybrids, pink

Ranunculus, Hadeco hybrids, orange

Rhodohypoxis baurii 'Apple Blossom'

used in bedding schemes and to add color to perennial borders. They are not long-lasting in flower, and in the garden should be replaced by other plants once they have passed their peak.

RHODOHYPOXIS

A genus of one to three species from South Africa. They are relatively winter-hardy, as long as they are kept on the dry side. They flower from spring through summer and sometimes into fall. The light brown to yellow rootstock is cormlike and about ½ in. (12 mm) across. The plants are very dwarf, seldom reaching more than 3 in. (7.5 cm). The flat, narrow, hairy leaves are produced in early spring and sheathe one another at the base. The white forms seem to produce fewer leaves than the pink and red ones.

Peaty, well-drained soil, in sun, ample moisture in spring and summer but not waterlogged. Zones 8–9.

Plant in fall, 1 in. (2.5 cm) deep, 3–5 in. (7.5–12.5 cm) apart.

Rhodohypoxis baurii (Jack Hobbs)

Use in bold masses in the rock garden and sunny borders. Due to their short stems, these showy flowers should be planted where their beauty can be easily seen and appreciated. Rock gardeners often grow them in troughs.

Rhodohypoxis baurii. Red star. South Africa, Lesotho. Rootstock cormlike, light-colored, cylindrical. Leaves 6–10, flat, pointed, very hairy, about 3 in. (7.5 cm) long. Flowers solitary on stiff, hairy pedicels, to 1½ in. (4 cm) across; color varies from white to deep pink and red; summer. Capsules develop just below the flat flowers. Stamens hidden. **'Apple Blossom'**, flowers 1 in. (2.5 cm) across, pale pink with darker center. **Var. *confecta***, flowers white to red, often aging to red. **Var. *platypetala***, occurs in drier sites, flowers white to pale pink, leaves broader.

Rhodohypoxis rubella. South Africa, Lesotho. Similar to *R. baurii* but scape hairless and leaves narrower, more cylindrical, and less hairy. Flowers pink.

ROMULEA

A genus of about 90 species closely related to *Crocus* and distributed in western Europe, Great Britain, and the Mediterranean; and in South Africa at higher elevations. *Romulea* species are seldom taller than 6 in. (15 cm). The corm has a shiny brown tunic and a characteristic small "foot," like a reduced version of the foot on a *Colchicum* corm. The leaves are few (up to six, usually two) and, unlike those of *Crocus*, do not have a white central stripe. The upward-facing flowers, which last four or five days, open only in bright sunlight and close in late afternoon—another reason these spring-flowering bulbs are best suited to mild regions with warm, sunny spring days. They have six tepals of similar size and shape. Colors include white, pink, purple, red, blue, and yellow, often with one or two zones of contrasting colors in the center.

Blooms spring or early summer.

Well-drained, moderately humus-rich, sandy soil, in full sun, moisture in winter and early spring, dry in summer. Zones 8–10.

Plant in early fall, 2 in. (5 cm) deep, 3–4 in. (7.5–10 cm) apart.

Use in masses in the rock garden and the front of the border, especially in mild areas. A good container plant. Keep somewhere warm and sunny to prolong flowering. Because it closes early in the afternoon, it does not make a good house plant.

Romulea rosea. South Africa. Plant height 6–8 in. (15–20 cm). Leaves narrow, 10–12 in. (25–30 cm) long. Flowers 1½ in. (4 cm) across, satiny pink to purple with maroon blotches above yellow central zone; winter to early spring. Relatively hardy. **Var.** *australis*, pale lilac-pink. **Var.** *elegans*, white with a yellow throat, outer segments red, red-purple, or red-green on outside.

Var. *reflexa*, magenta to pink-lilac, occasionally white, throat orange-yellow often with violet-blue zone.

Romulea tabularis. South Africa. Plant height to 3 in. (7.5 cm). Flowers bluish with yellow center surrounded with white, winter to early spring.

Sandersonia aurantiaca
Chinese lantern, Christmas bells

South Africa. Rootstock a fleshy, small, fingerlike, very brittle tuber. Stems thin, wiry, scrambling or semi-erect, to about 2 ft. (60 cm). Leaves bright green, to 3 in. (7.5 cm) long, lance-shaped, tapering to a fine point which may extend into a tendril to help the plant scramble through shrubs.

Romulea rosea
(Robert Ornduff)

Romulea tabularis
(Robert Ornduff)

Flowers large, bright orange, bell-shaped, pendent on short, curving pedicels arising from the axils of the upper leaves; mid summer. Perianth segments six, fused; stamens hidden inside the flower. A spur which points toward the mouth is found on the exterior of the flower near the base of each segment; this is the pitted channel from the nectary gland inside.

Blooms mid summer.

Well-drained, moisture-retentive, humus-rich soil, in full sun in all but the hottest regions, where it appreciates light afternoon shade. Give ample moisture at planting time, with increasing moisture as the foliage develops. Leave plants undisturbed for four or five years. In fall the plants should be drier, but never without a little moisture in the soil. In a cold greenhouse, plants can perform well for many years. Zones 9–10.

Plant in late winter a few weeks before the last frost, about 3 in. (7.5 cm) deep, in soil improved to a depth of 18 in. (45 cm) plant. Handle fragile tubers with care.

Use as a container plant in colder climates; bring indoors and protect from frost. Grow outdoors in warmer climates, staked so the flowers can be seen to advantage

Sauromatum venosum
Monarch of the East, voodoo lily

Himalaya, southern India. Tuber rounded, to 6 in. (15 cm) across or more. Leaf stalk to 18 in. (45

Sandersonia aurantiaca (Chris Lovell)

Sauromatum venosum (Katarina Stenman)

cm) long, thick at base, often brown-spotted. Leaf solitary, round, deeply divided into 8- to 10-in. (20- to 25-cm) segments, which are sometimes further divided. Flower stalk short; spathe up to 2 ft. (60 cm) long; tubular lower part hides the female flowers, then splits and unfolds with the sharply pointed spathe curling back and twisting, displaying mottled interior of spathe, purplish and green with darker purple blotches. Flowers stink like decaying flesh.

Blooms late spring or early summer.

Well-drained, humus-rich soil, in bright (not direct) sunlight, ample moisture as the spathe emerges, keeping moist until the leaf has died down. Requires warmth year-round. Zones 9–10.

Plant tubers 3–4 in. (7.5–10 cm) deep.

Use in tropical gardens with high humidity and heat, or in a warm greenhouse. Although not of great beauty, this species is unusual because the big tuber can produce the very large inflorescence without being planted in soil.

Var. *pedatum*, a green, unspotted leaf stalk and shorter spathe, yellowish and purple.

Scadoxus multiflorus
Blood lily

South Africa. Bulbs large, fleshy. Roots brittle, thick. Stems to 2 ft. (60 cm). Leaves 7–10, to 18 in. (45 cm) long, very wide at the base, elongating after flowering. Flowers deep scarlet, umbel to 10 in. (25 cm) across.

Blooms summer, sometimes only in alternate years.

Well-drained, humus-rich soil, in full sun but preferring some shade, ample water when growing but dry when dormant. Little fertilizer is needed unless the plants have been growing in the same spot for several years; then give weak feedings of liquid organic fertilizer every two or three weeks. Zones 9–11.

Plant bulbs with the neck just at or a little above soil level, about 12 in. (30 cm) apart, in groups of three or five. Take care not to break the fleshy roots. Pots should be at least 10 in. (25 cm) across.

Scadoxus multiflorus subsp. *katherinae*

Use for its attractive flowers: small, with colorful stamens crowded together, having the form of a shaving brush, and with up to 100 flowers per inflorescence.

Subsp. *katherinae*. Catherine wheel, blood flower. The tallest subspecies; it has scarlet flowers with very prominent stamens.

Subsp. *longitubus* is the shortest subspecies and has flowers with perianth tube up to 1 in. (2.5 cm) long.

Schizostylis coccinea
Coffee lily, crimson flag

South Africa, Swaziland, and Zimbabwe. Rootstock a fleshy rhizome. Stems to 20 in. (50 cm). Leaves long and grasslike, sheathing base of stem. Flowers satin-textured, pale scarlet, narrowly tubular at base, opening flat; pointed tepals produce a starry form. Stamens attached in throat.

Blooms late summer to fall, with a few flowers in spring.

Well-drained soil, keep dry after the foliage has died down. Zones 6–10.

Plant in early fall, 2 in. (5 cm) deep, 6–8 in. (15–20 cm) apart.

Use as container plants for the cool greenhouse. Must be protected from frost while in leaf. In mild climates, they are useful in the sunny, well-drained border and should be placed where night-blooming habit and fragrance can be appreciated.

Schizostylis coccinea (International Flower Bulb Center)

'**Alba**', white flushed pink.

'**Major**', larger flowers of clearer red.

'**Mrs. Hegarty**', rose pink.

'**Oregon Sunset**', orange-red, providing excellent color into early November, spreading to form large colonies.

'**Rosea**', rose pink.

'**Sunrise**', pink.

'**Viscountess Byng**', pale shell pink, flowering into November.

SCILLA
Squill

A genus of about 100 species distributed throughout the Old World in tropical and temperate areas, from South Africa to the Mediterranean, Europe, Great Britain, and Asia. *Scilla* species may flower in spring, summer, or fall, but those most common in gardens are all spring blooming. The tunicated bulb is composed of nu-merous free scales which are renewed annually. The flowers are small and starry, few to many in a raceme. The leaves are linear to lance-shaped and are all basal.

Fast-draining, humus-rich soil, with light shade in hot regions and full sun in cool ones, moderate moisture until the foliage withers.

Plant *Scilla peruviana* and *S. natalensis* with the top of the bulb at or above soil level, the other species 3–4 in. (7.5–10 cm) deep, 3–12 in. (7.5–30 cm) apart, depending on the species.

Use in any garden. In warmer climates, *Scilla peruviana* and *S. natalensis* are good border plants. *Scilla siberica* is the most popular one in cold-winter regions and is a good companion to early daffodils. The smaller species are appropriate for the rock garden. Most should be planted in large groups for best effect.

Scilla bifolia. Europe, Turkey. Stems 2–4 in. (5–10 cm), elongating in fruit. Leaves usually

Scilla bifolia

Scilla natalensis (Harry B. Hay)

Scilla miczenkoana, white form (International Flower Bulb Center)

Scilla peruviana

two, sometimes four. Flowers to eight per stem, 1 in. (2.5 cm) across, outward- or upward-facing, usually bright blue, sometimes paler; early spring. A fine early bulb, in its native habitat flowering soon after the snow melts. Plant in cool spots in hot-summer climates. Zones 6–9.

Scilla miczenkoana. Iran, Caucasus. Stems three or four per bulb, each to 6 in. (15 cm) tall. Leaves broader than those of many spring-flowering scillas. Flowers three to five per stem, flat-faced, light blue with darker median stripe, late winter or early spring. Zone 6.

Scilla natalensis. Blue squill, tall squill. South Africa, Lesotho. Bulb very large, with purplish-brown tunic; plant with upper third above soil level. Stems often over 3 ft. (90 cm). Leaves develop after flowering begins, often 4 in. (10 cm) wide or more, up to 18 in. (45 cm) long, green on upper surface, sometimes flushed purple on underside. Flowers to 100 on long horizontal pedicels in well-spaced, pyramidal raceme, powder blue to lavender blue; lower parts of segments fused into a narrow tube, separating to a flat-faced flower; spring. Zone 9. A striking plant, ideal species for setting between boulders; grow frost-free. Prefers full sun, well-drained soil, and ample moisture when growing. **Var.** *sordida*, leaves tinged brown, more slender leafless flower stalk.

Scilla peruviana. Cuban lily, Peruvian lily. Portugal, Spain, and Italy. Stems to 12 in. (30 cm), elongating during flowering period. Leaves nearly evergreen, in a basal rosette, to 1 1/2 in. (4 cm) wide, 12 in. (30 cm) long. Flowers to 100 in dense raceme, deep violet blue; inflorescence to 6 in. (15 cm) across, with lower flowers on pedicels 1 1/2 in. (4 cm) long, upper pedicels very short. In seed, pedicels almost double their length; late spring. Excellent container plant for colder regions, wintered under glass and brought outside after last frost. Plant bulb with the neck at soil level. Zones 8–11. **'Alba'**, white. **'Elegans'**, red. **Var.** *glabra*, lilac, leaves smooth.

Scilla peruviana 'Alba'

Scilla siberica. Siberian squill. Iran, Turkey, Caucasus. Stems to 8 in. (20 cm), frequently more than one per bulb. Leaves four to six, narrow, bright green, to 8 in. (20 cm) long. Flowers to six per stem, brilliant blue, often facing one direction, somewhat pendent, to 1 in. (2.5 cm) across; mid spring. Zones 2–8. **'Spring Beauty'**, deep blue. **Var. *taurica***, darker blue flowers that appear slightly earlier than the type. Very popular in gardens.

SPARAXIS
Harlequin flower, wand flower

This genus of about 14 species from South Africa includes some of the brightest bulbous flowers. The rootstock is a corm with a fibrous tunic. The pale green, flat, stiff, and tough leaves are held in a fan at the base of the stem. The flowers are quite large, many on the stem, which is sometimes branched; each flower has a separate spathe. A wide range of colors exists, especially among the many hybrids. The center of the flower is cup-shaped, and the tepals spread to a diameter often exceeding 3 in. (7.5 cm). There are six perianth segments, more or less equal. The stamens are short, arising from the base of the cup.

Blooms spring or early summer.

Well-drained, loamy soil, in full sun, moisture until the foliage matures, then dry. Zones 9–10.

Plant in fall, 2 in. (5 cm) deep, 3–4 in. (7.5–10 cm) apart.

Use in groups of 25 or more in gardens with mild winters. Excellent in containers and for long-lasting cut flowers. These plants have not enjoyed the popularity they deserve. With their various color combinations, they are bright, cheerful plants of easy culture that deserve to be more widely grown in any sunny, well-drained border, among rocks and other areas where they can remain dry in late summer. They are good pot plants for the cool greenhouse in cooler areas and ideal plants for planting in stone walls.

Sparaxis elegans. South Africa. Stems 10–12 in. (25–30 cm), unbranched, up to five per corm. Leaves slender, swordlike, in a basal fan, to 8 in. (20 cm) long. Flowers up to three per stem, about

Sparaxis grandiflora

1½ in. (4 cm) across, salmon pink or white with purplish center, the white sometimes flushed blue; anthers curled and twisted around style; late spring. **'Coccinea'**, glowing orange-red flowers with near-black center. **'Zwanenburg'**, maroon-red flowers with yellow centers.

Sparaxis grandiflora. South Africa. Stems to 12 in. (30 cm), more in cultivars. Leaves usually two, narrow, rarely more than ½ in. (12 mm) wide, to 8 in. (20 cm) long, carried close to the stem. Flowers may be plum-colored, the largest in the genus—often 3 in. (7.5 cm) across, mid to late spring.

Sparaxis tricolor. South Africa. Stems 10–12 in. (25–30 cm), up to five produced by one corm. Leaves generally four or five, stiff, in a fan, ⅓ in. (8 mm) wide and 6–8 in. (15–20 cm) long. Flowers two to five per stem, spectacularly colored orange, with deep yellow centers outlined with black; late spring. **'Fire King'**, brilliant scarlet flowers with yellow centers and flowering later. **'Mixed'** includes selections chosen for wide color range and long flowering period as well as vigor.

STERNBERGIA
Autumn daffodil

A genus of about eight species from the Mediterranean and Middle East, often growing in rocky places. The flowers at first glance resemble those of *Crocus*. All but two species are fall-flowering, and all but one have yellow flowers. They are small plants, rarely more than 6 in. (15 cm) high. The dark, tunicated bulbs are poisonous if eaten, to 2 in. (5 cm) across, and produce lax, narrow leaves. The flowers are usually solitary, but the bulbs offset and form clusters, so the floral display can be quite showy. Some species open their flowers nearly at ground level, others on a relatively short aboveground stem. The six perianth segments are fused at the base into a narrow tube, short or long depending on the species. The seeds are either dark brown or black.

Well-drained, moderately fertile soil, in full sun, moisture in fall and winter, hot and dry in summer. Zones 7–9.

Plant in late summer, 6 in. (15 cm) deep, 4–6 in. (10–15 cm) apart.

Sparaxis tricolor

Use for its superb golden yellow flowers in fall. Put in the front of the border, provided they receive a hot, dry summer dormancy there. They are expensive to purchase, however, since they do not increase rapidly, and the entire genus is listed as endangered by the Convention on International Trade in Endangered Species (CITES).

Sternbergia colchiflora. Spain, Italy, and Balkans. Stems below ground level. Leaves narrow, deep green or grayish, present at flowering and elongating later. Flowers pale yellow, sweet-scented, narrow, just over 1 in. (2.5 cm) long, late summer to early fall.

Sternbergia lutea. Lily-of-the-field, Mount Etna lily. Spain to Iran and Central Asia. Bulb similar to a *Narcissus* bulb, with dark tunic. Stems 3–8 in. (7.5–20 cm). Leaves four to six, present at flowering and elongating later, 6–10 in. (15–25 cm) long, ½ in. (12 mm) wide. Flowers rich golden yellow, egg-shaped, to 2 in. (5 cm) long and as wide. The most commonly grown sternbergia, perhaps the best of fall-flowering bulbs. 'Angustifolia', narrower leaves.

Sternbergia lutea
(International Flower Bulb Center)

Tigridia pavonia, red form
(Jack Hobbs)

Tigridia pavonia
Peacock flower, tiger flower

Mexico. Rootstock an ovoid corm, covered with a coarse tunic. Stems usually 18–20 in. (45–50 cm). Leaves sword-shaped, 10–12 in. (25–30 cm) long; the few stem leaves arranged in a fan. Flower spikes surpassed by tops of the foliage but never hidden. Flowers 2–4 in. (5–10 cm), yellow, white, red, or orange, usually with purplish spots or blotches in cup, held in a spathe. Flowers short lived, but the plants are free-flowering.

Blooms summer.

Well-drained soil, in full sun, adequate moisture when growing, gradually reducing water after the foliage starts to turn brown. Zone 5.

Plant in spring, 3–4 in. (7.5–10 cm) deep, 6–10 in. (15–25 cm) apart.

Use for summer color in all sunny borders. Place among other plants whose foliage will cover the rather sparse *Tigridia* foliage. The background fill adds much to the appreciation of the bright flowers. With their ease of culture it is surprising tigridias are not more widely grown.

'**Alba Grandiflora**', white with dark red spots.

Tigridia pavonia, white form (Jack Hobbs)

Tigridia pavonia, yellow form (Jack Hobbs)

Trillium grandiflorum

'**Alba Immaculata**', white without spots.

'**Aurea**', dark golden yellow with red spots.

'**Canariensis**', creamy yellow with carmine splashes.

'**Liliacea**', reddish purple variegated white.

TRILLIUM
Wood lily, wake robin

A genus of about 44 species, most of which are from eastern North America, with a few species in western North America and in far eastern Asia. Trilliums are among the finest woodland plants, a symbol of spring to Americans. The rhizome is cylindrical, often knobby, very tough, generally dark, and may be more than 1 in. (2.5 cm) across. The three broadly elliptical leaves are held horizontally in a whorl near the top of the stem. The flowers range from about 1 in. (2.5 cm) to more than 4 in. (10 cm) across and are solitary, held above the leaf whorl. In some species the flowers are upward-facing, and in others pendent. The sessile types usually have leaves mottled light and dark in an irregular pattern, making them even more ornamental. Only one set of leaves and a single flower are carried on a stem, but a large rhizome may produce more than one stem. The three outer segments (the sepals) are always green and pointed. The three inner segments (petals) are more conspicuous and may be white, pale yellow, purple, or reddish, sometimes erect and sometimes spreading horizontally. There are six stamens; the style is cleft or three-branched from the base.

Blooms early spring to early summer.

Friable, humus-rich loam, dappled shade, moderate moisture year-round.

Plant in late summer or fall, 4 in. (10 cm) deep, 8–12 in. (20–30 cm) apart.

Use in bold groups in moist woodlands. Great garden plants; ideal among azaleas and low-growing rhododendrons as they like the same conditions. Trilliums with upward-facing flowers must be viewed from above, and those with pendent flowers are pleasing on a high bank. Plants

Trillium sessile

tolerate gentle forcing, when moisture is provided and temperatures are near 55°F (13°C) at night.

Trillium erectum. Red trillium, birth-root. Eastern North America. Stems to 12 in. (30 cm), often more than one per rhizome. Leaves stalkless, broadly rhomboidal and narrowing abruptly. Flowers on stalks, usually reddish, rarely white, yellow, or green, 1 in. (2.5 cm) long, 1½ in. (4 cm) across; flower stalk to 3 in. (7.5 cm) long, bent sharply just above base of flower; mid to late spring. Zones 4–9. **'Albiflorum'**, white stained green. **'Luteum'**, green-yellow below, blood-red above.

Trillium grandiflorum. Great white trillium, snow lily. Eastern North America. Stems 12–18 in. (30–45 cm). Flowers on stalks, white, rarely pink, funnel-form with arching flower stalks, almost outward-facing, often more than 3 in. (7.5 cm) across when fully open; petals to 2 in. (5 cm) long; mid to late spring. Possibly the finest species of the genus. Zones 5–9. **'Flore Pleno'**, double. **Forma** *parvum*, smaller flowers fading to violet-pink. **'Roseum'** (or f. *roseum*), clear pink. **Forma** *variegatum*, white-margined leaves.

Trillium sessile. Toadshade. Eastern United States. Stems 10–12 in. (25–30 cm). Leaves about 3 in. (7.5 cm) long and as broad, mottled light and dark green. Flowers stalkless, dark crimson; petals 1½ in. (4 cm) long. Most attractive when planted in bold groups. Zones 4–9. **Forma** *viridiflorum*, smaller yellow flowers.

TRITELEIA
Grass nuts

A genus of 13 species from western United States, closely related to *Dichelostemma*. The corm is flattened and covered with a light-colored fibrous tunic. The stem is leafless and sometimes hairy at the base. The one or two leaves are linear, dark shiny green, and V-shaped in cross section, with a prominent midrib below. The flowers, borne in an umbel, have a fairly short, funnel-shaped tube and six flaring lobes. There are six fertile stamens, with flattened, threadlike filaments that may be equal

Triteleia ixioides 'Starlight' (International Flower Bulb Center)

or unequal. The stigma is small, and the style slender. Most species have blue to violet flowers; a few are white or yellow.

In full sun, moderate moisture in fall and spring.

Plant 4–5 in. (10–12.5 cm) deep, 6 in. (15 cm) apart.

Use in groups of five to seven among rocks or in dry grassland, where they may naturalize and increase. Suited to dry borders and sunny openings in woodland. They grow well in containers, but most are not pleasing as pot plants owing to the absence of foliage at flowering time. They are good cut flowers and can be dried for winter arrangements.

Triteleia ixioides (syn. *Brodiaea ixioides*). Golden star, pretty face. Stems to 20 in. (50 cm). Leaves fleshy, linear, 3–8 in. (7.5–20 cm) long. Flowers few to 20, on pedicles 1 1/2 in. (4 cm) long, about 1 in. (2.5 cm) across, pale to deep with purple or brown median stripes; tube rarely more than 1/4 in. (6 mm) long; late spring. Zones 7–10, **Var. *anilina***, dull yellow flowers with blue anthers. **Var. *scabra***, pale yellow flowers, cream to yellow anthers; **'Starlight'**, very floriferous.

Triteleia laxa (syn. *Brodiaea laxa*). Grass nuts, triplet lily. Stems 8–24 in. (20–60 cm). Leaves 1–2 ft. (30–60 cm) long, linear, pointed. Flowers in loose umbel on 2-in. (5-cm) pedicels, often more than 1 in. (2.5 cm) across and 1 1/2 in. (4 cm) long, pale to deep violet-blue; early summer. Stamens attached at two levels; anthers blue. The most commonly grown species and a good cut flower. Zones 6–9. **'Humboldt Star'**, similar but flowers a bit larger; **'Koningin Fabiola'** ("Queen Fabiola"), a little taller than the species, with stronger stems, 25 or more medium violet-blue flowers per stem.

TRITONIA
Blazing star, montbretia
A genus of about 28 species from tropical Africa and South Africa. The rootstock is a corm with a thin, dry, fibrous tunic 1/2 in. (12 mm) across— much smaller than one would expect from the size of the plants, whose stems can reach 2 ft.

Triteleia laxa 'Koningin Fabiola' (International Flower Bulb Center)

(60 cm). Sword-shaped leaves, rigid and varying in width, are arranged fanlike in equal ranks on either side of the stalk. The stem emerges from between the leaves and generally exceeds them in length; it may be branched and may have a single stem leaf. Heights range from 6 in. (15 cm) to more than 24 in. (60 cm). The number of flowers produced is never fewer than six, except from immature corms. The flowers are stalkless. The base is a narrow tube, and the perianth segments flare to a bowl shape and recurve at the tips. On each of the lower three tepals is a structure like a little vertical post or horn, often contrastingly colored. The flowers are arranged alternately on opposite sides of the stem, producing a zigzag effect, but may all turn to one side as they open. Colors are mostly in orange to red, but other colors occur, especially in hybrids. All species flower over a long period.

Blooms summer.

Well-drained soil, moisture when growing, dry when the leaves begin to turn brown. Zones 8–10.

Tritonia crocata (Jack Hobbs)

Tritonia hybrids (Jack Hobbs)

In colder areas, plant two or three weeks before the last frost; elsewhere, plant early summer-flowering species in fall, late summer-flowering species in spring. Set corms 2 in. (5 cm) deep and 4–6 in. (10–15 cm) apart.

Use in milder climates, in bold groups. Ideal for the sunny border. The smaller species are best in the rock garden.

Tritonia crocata. Orange freesia. South Africa. Stems 4–15 in. (10–37.5 cm). Leaves usually four or more, stiff, pointed, sword-shaped, in a basal fan, shorter than the stem. Flowers held erect, somewhat bowl-shaped, 1 1/2 in. (4 cm) across, orange to reddish; late spring to early summer. The most common species. **'Baby Doll'**, salmon. **'Bridal Veil'**, white. **'Pink Sensation'**, pink. **'Serendipity'**, light red. **'Tangerine'**, orange.

Tritonia flabellifolia. South Africa. Stems to 12 in. (30 cm). Flowers white, spring to early summer.

Tropaeolum tuberosum
Garden nasturtium

Andes of Bolivia and Peru. Rootstock a large, yellow tuber. Stems purplish red, climbing to 10 ft. (3 m). Leaves rounded, notched, with five lobes, no lobes or teeth on lower part of blade. Flower cup-shaped, colorful; sepals five, red; petals five, yellow or reddish; spur to 1 in. (2.5 cm) long. other in summer.

Blooms mid summer.

Best in extremely well drained, acidic soils, in full sun, ample moisture when growing but drought-tolerant when dormant. If fertilized, they make abundant vegetative growth at the expense of flowering. They normally go dormant in late summer or fall, but in warm climates they may be almost evergreen, with only a short dormancy, if any. Zones 8–10.

Plant 4–5 in. (10–12.5 cm) deep, 10 ft. (3 m) apart.

Use in gardens where it can be supported on a trellis. Often grown through shrubs. Can be grown in large containers, where the plant is allowed to trail.

'Ken Aslet', light orange.

Tropaeolum tuberosum (International Flower Bulb Center)

Tulbaghia violacea
Society garlic, pink agapanthus

South Africa. Roots fat, tuberous. Leaves green, shiny, 8–12 in. (20–30 cm) long, forming a tuft out of which stem emerges. Stems 8–14 in. (20–35 cm). Flowers to 20 per umbel, mauve, long-lasting.

Blooms spring and summer.

Well-drained soil, in full sun, moisture while the foliage is developing but largely withheld as soon as the flower spikes appear. Little or no feeding required, but established plants benefit from a general fertilizer when growth starts. Zones 7–10.

Plant in spring, 1–2 in. (2.5–5 cm) deep, 6–12 in. (15–30 cm) apart.

Use in sunny borders in warm areas, in the cool greenhouse in colder regions. Best in masses. Frequently used as a bedding plant in South African gardens, parks, and street landscaping. In the

Tulbaghia violacea

wild, it is just as attractive, forming colonies of considerable size close to the seashore. Very easy culture.

TULIPA
Tulip

A genus of about 100 species and many thousands of cultivars from Europe, Asia, and North Africa. The flowers of almost all species are relatively large and bright, and most species are fairly cold hardy. The bulbs have tunics which may be lined with hairs, or "wool," especially in species from very cold, dry areas. The leaves are linear to broadly elliptical or lance-shaped. The flowers are usually solitary, but in some species and cultivars two or three flowers are borne on short branches. The flowers are mostly erect, rarely nodding, and bell- or funnel-shaped. The tepals are separate for their entire length and usually have a contrastingly colored blotch at the base, most often yellow but sometimes whitish; there may also be a black central zone. There are six stamens. The ovary is three-celled, and the stigma cleft into three.

Blooms spring to early summer, depending on the species and cultivars.

Well-drained soil, in full sun but tolerate light shade, moisture but not waterlogged. Fertilize as soon as the foliage appears if bulbs are to be saved for subsequent years. Hardiness varies by species, Zones 6–9 for cultivars.

Plant in fall at least 6 in. (15 cm) deep, 8 in. (20 cm) deep in sandy soil, 5 in. (12.5 cm) in sandy soils, 6–8 in. (15–20 cm) apart.

Use in borders, beds, containers, and rock gardens—almost everywhere except woodland. They make excellent cut flowers, amenable to forcing, and should be in every garden.

Tulipa acuminata. Horned tulip. Turkey. Stems to 18 in. (45 cm). Flowers yellow and red;

Tulipa acuminata

tepals twisted with threadlike tips, 3–4 in. (7.5–10 cm) long; late spring. Possibly an old Turkish garden form. Zones 3–8.

Tulipa clusiana. Lady tulip, candy-stick tulip. Iran, Iraq, Afghanistan. Stems to 12 in. (30 cm) or more. Leaves four, lower two folded, 8–10 in. (20–25 cm) long, ½ in. (12 mm) wide. Flowers solitary, flat, starry when fully open; interior white with dark blue basal zone; exterior red edged in white; tepals 2 in. (5 cm) long, ³⁄4 in. (2 cm) wide, pointed; mid to late spring. Zones 3–8. **Var. *chrysantha*** has golden yellow tepals, exterior stained red or purple-brown. **Var. *chrysantha* 'Tubergen's Gem'**, large flowers. **'Cynthia'**, cream flowers, red on exterior. **Var. *stellata***, a yellow basal blotch.

Tulipa fosteriana. Uzbekistan. Stems 6–18 in. (15–45 cm). Leaves three, lowest to 8 in. (20 cm) long, 4 in. (10 cm) wide. Flowers bright scarlet with black, yellow-edged basal blotch;

Tulipa clusiana (Harry B. Hay)

Tulipa 'Purissima', Fosteriana Group

Tulipa 'Golden Emperor', Fosteriana Group
(Jack Hobbs)

Tulipa greigii hybrid, in a container

Tulipa 'Red Emperor', Fosteriana Group

Tulipa greigii 'Plaisir'

outer tepals often over 3 in. (7.5 cm) long; inner segments a little shorter, half as wide as long, blunt-pointed; early to mid spring. Zones 5–8.

Tulipa greigii. Turkestan. Stems 16–18 in. (40–45 cm). Leaves three or four per bulb, 3–4 in. (7.5–10 cm) wide, grayish, mottled or striped purple-brown stripes or mottled, lowest to 8 in. (20 cm) long. Flowers solitary, cup-shaped, scar- let with dark blotch on bright yellow base; outer tepals over 3 in. (7.5 cm) long, 2 in. (5 cm) wide, curled back; inner tepals remain erect; mid spring. Much used in hybridizing. All the Greigii selections and hybrids have a trace of purple-brown or pinkish variegation on foliage and bloom in April. The very large, cup-shaped flowers, often more than 5 in. (12.5 cm) across, and the crimson-variegated grayish leaves make very

Tulipa saxatilis (Harry B. Hay)

Tulipa 'Apricot Beauty', Single Early Group

Tulipa 'Kees Nelis', Triumph Group (Jack Hobbs)

Tulipa 'Atilla', Triumph Group (Jack Hobbs)

attractive plants in garden or containers. The tepals are often differently colored outside and inside. Zones 5–8.

Tulipa saxatilis. Candia tulip. Crete. Bulb stoloniferous, tunic yellow-brown tinged pink. Stems 6–8 in. (15–20 cm). Leaves 6–12 in. (15–30 cm) long, flat, shiny green. Flowers fragrant, one to four per stem, cup-shaped, pale lilac with yellow blotch; tepals 2 in. (5 cm) long, 1 in. (2.5 cm) wide. Zones 6–8.

Tulip hybrids are divided into various groups, several of which are illustrated here. **Single Early Group**: the earliest to bloom, starting in March to mid-April, generally 6–8 in. (15–20 cm) tall, good for edging beds filled with annuals, especially in windswept areas where taller-growing types might be damaged. **Triumph Group**: stems 18–24 in. (45–60 cm) tall, stiff, and strong; great for outdoors. **Darwin Hybrid Group**: flowers large, up to 7 in. (17.5 cm) across in cup form, 12 in. (30 cm) across when open flat toward the end of blooming, mostly red and

Tulipa 'Negrita', Triumph Group (Jack Hobbs)

Tulipa 'Appledorn's Elite', Darwin Hybrid Group

Tulipa 'Oxford', Darwin Hybrid Group (Jack Hobbs)

Tulipa 'Oxford's Elite', Darwin Hybrid Group, at Wellington Botanic Garden (Jack Hobbs)

Tulipa 'Georgette', Single Late Group

Tulipa 'West Point', Lily-flowered Group

Tulipa 'Greenland', Viridiflora Group

Tulipa 'Carnaval de Nice', Double Late Group

Tulips and primulas (Jack Hobbs)

Tulipa 'Flaming Parrot', Parrot Group (Jack Hobbs)

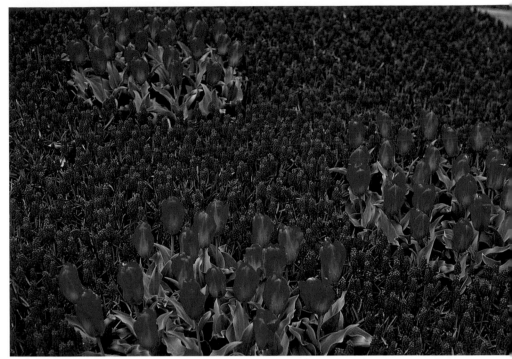

Tulips and grape hyacinths

yellow, excellent as cut flowers; stems up to 28 in. (70 cm) tall. **Single Late Group**: flowers usually rectangular, with rounded, satiny tepals and flat-topped buds, blooming in late April or early May; stems generally 26–32 in. (65–80 cm) tall; very resistant to wind and rain; ideal for bedding; excellent as cut flowers. **Lily-flowered Group**: flower lilylike with very pointed, reflexed tepals, blooming late April to early May; stems around 2 ft. (60 cm) tall; excellent in borders and as long-lasting cut flowers. **Viridiflora Group**: exotic-looking flowers with varying amounts of green in the tepals or midveins; much in demand by florists. **Parrot Group**: flowers fringed, tepal edges finely shredded, scalloped, or undulating; blooming in May; stems 20–24 in. (50–60 cm). tall; good cut flower. **Double Late (Peony-flowered) Group**: flowers large, often the last to bloom in mid to late May; need protection from wind and rain; stems 16–24 in. (40–60 cm) tall; good in containers.

Veltheimia bracteata
Red-hot poker

South Africa. Bulb large, fleshy, to 6 in. (15 cm) across. Stems mottled with purple, 18–20 in. (45–50 cm). Leaves about 10 in a basal rosette, to 18 in. (45 cm) long and 4 in. (10 cm) wide, with undulating margins, deep shiny green sometimes flecked with pale green, well-developed at flowering time. Flowers drooping, often more than 50 in dense raceme, tubular, almost 2 in. (5 cm) long, pale rose flecked at tip with green.

Blooms mid winter to early spring.

Well-drained soil, in shade (never exposed to hot sun), adequate moisture from fall to spring, with a dry period in summer, but should never become completely dry. Give established plants slow-release or liquid organic fertilizer while in growth. Zones 10–11.

Plant bulbs with their tops 1–2 in. (2.5–5 cm) below the soil surface, 6–10 in. (15–25 cm) apart. Root disturbance inhibits flowering.

Veltheimia bracteata (Jack Hobbs)

Use in shady gardens in warm areas. Excellent container plants in mild climates, for the cool greenhouse, or indoors. Robust yet fragile-looking, charming. Foliage ornamental, flowers long-lasting.

WATSONIA
Bugle flower, bugle lily

A genus of many species from South Africa, Lesotho, and Swaziland. Relatively trouble-free and easy to grow.

Blooms spring or summer, depending on the species.

Well-drained, humus-rich soil, moisture in winter and spring if spring-flowering, in summer if summer-flowering. Zones 8–10.

Plant in fall if spring-flowering, in spring if summer-flowering, 2–3 in. (5–7.5 cm) deep, 6–10 in. (15–25 cm) apart.

Use for summer bedding plants, like gladioli. All watsonias are good subjects for the cool greenhouse, either in open borders or in containers. They are good cut flowers. Plant the taller species in shrub borders where their flower spikes will rise above low-growing plants and prolong interest.

Watsonia borbonica. South Africa. Stems branched, often over 5 ft. (1.5 m). Leaves 30 in. (75 cm) long, 1 in. (2.5 cm) wide. Flowers cyclamen pink, over 2 in. (5 cm) in diameter; tube 1 in. (2.5 cm) long. Flowering spring to early summer; dormant in summer. **Subsp.** *ardernei* is slightly smaller, with pure white flowers which appear a bit earlier.

Watsonia meriana. South Africa. Stems 2–3 ft. (60–90 cm). Leaves 1–2 ft. (30–60 cm) long, to ½ in. (12 mm) wide. Flowers white, pink, or mauve; tube about 2 in. (5 cm) long, lobes spreading to over 2 in. (5 cm) across; spring. **'Bulbillifera'**, stems 5 ft. (1.5 m), has fewer but larger orange flowers; produces bulbils in axils of bracts and stem leaves.

Watsonia borbonica subsp. *ardernei*

Watsonia meriana

Watsonia zeyheri, detail

Watsonia zeyheri

Watsonia zeyheri (syn. *W. comptonii*). South Africa. Stems to 3 ft. (90 cm). Leaves 24–30 in. (60–75 cm) long, ½ in. (12 mm) wide, evergreen. Flowers bright orange to apricot, arching up and away from stem, outward-facing, widely spaced; tube about 2 in. (5 cm) long; lobes flare to 1½ in. (4 cm) across; early summer.

ZANTEDESCHIA
Calla lily, arum lily

A genus of six or seven species from South Africa. The plants are produced from thick rhizomes. The leaf blade is arrow-shaped, sometimes variegated with white dots. The leaf stalks are long and thick and sheathe the stem base. The flowers are carried on a crowded spadix with no sterile flowers between the male and female flowers. The spathe is longer than the spadix and may be white, yellow, or rose, sometimes quite red. It is held erect, with a short tube, rolled together, and funnel-shaped; the blade is expanded and the tip curled back. Some species can reach over 6 ft. (1.8 m) in their native habitat, growing in wet, marshy ground, often on the edge of the forest.

Blooms spring to summer.

Humus-rich, moisture-retentive, wet soil, in sun or shade, moisture. Give heavy feedings of organic fertilizer. Zones 8–11.

Plant 4 in. (10 cm) deep, 12–18 in. (30–45 cm) apart.

Use in a border. Much used in the florist trade. Some have ornamentally variegated foliage and are attractive even when not in flower. For *Zantedeschia aethiopica*, the ideal location is on the edge of woods in rich soil with plenty of moisture. Other species are better suited for the greenhouse.

Zantedeschia aethiopica. Calla lily. Stems to 6 ft. (1.8 m) in native habitat, usually to 3 ft. (90 cm) in gardens. Leaves twice as long as broad, evergreen in warm climates, deciduous in colder areas. Spathe white, to 10 in. (25 cm) long, with margins curled back; spadix yellow; spring to early summer. The most commonly grown zantedeschia. If it likes its location, it soon forms large

Zantedeschia aethiopica, detail

Zantedeschia aethiopica

Zantedeschia elliotiana, detail

Zantedeschia elliotiana

Zantedeschia aethiopica 'Green Goddess'

clumps. **'Childsiana'**, a smaller form with more flowers. **'Crowborough'**, reputedly hardier than the type. **'Gigantea'**, a larger form. **'Green Goddess'**, with dull green leaves. **'Little Gem'**, a dwarf.

Zantedeschia elliotiana. Golden calla. Stems to 3 ft. (90 cm). Leaves blotched with silver, broad and heart-shaped at base. Spathe bright yellow, without blotch, to 6 in. (15 cm) long, summer.

USDA HARDINESS ZONE MAP

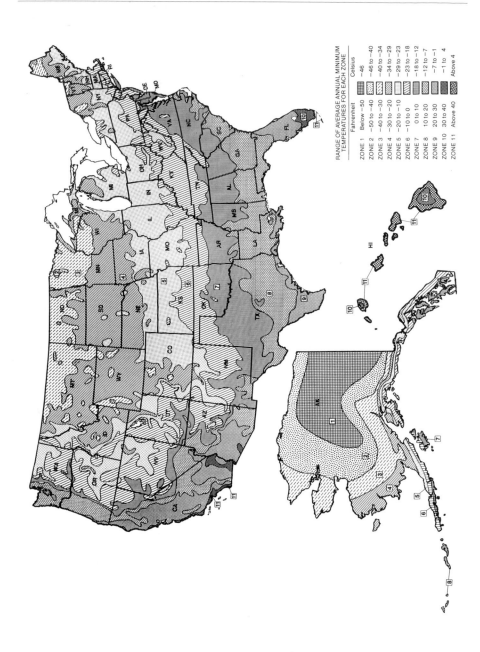

RANGE OF AVERAGE ANNUAL MINIMUM
TEMPERATURES FOR EACH ZONE

	Fahrenheit	Celsius
ZONE 1	Below −50	−46
ZONE 2	−50 to −40	−46 to −40
ZONE 3	−40 to −30	−40 to −34
ZONE 4	−30 to −20	−34 to −29
ZONE 5	−20 to −10	−29 to −23
ZONE 6	−10 to 0	−23 to −18
ZONE 7	0 to 10	−18 to −12
ZONE 8	10 to 20	−12 to −7
ZONE 9	20 to 30	−7 to −1
ZONE 10	30 to 40	−1 to 4
ZONE 11	Above 40	Above 4

EUROPEAN HARDINESS ZONE MAP

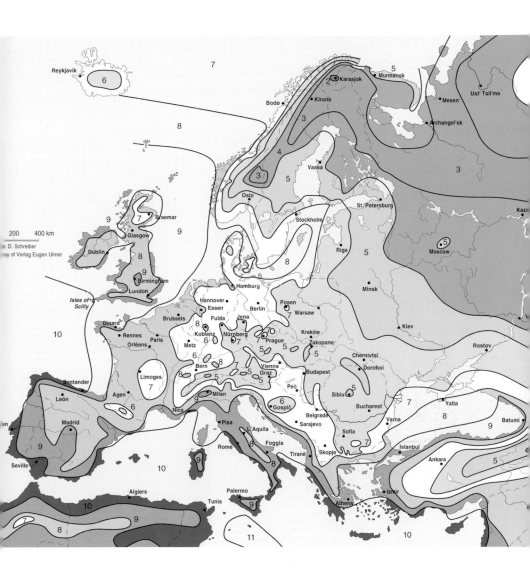

NURSERY SOURCES

This is a partial list, limited to nurseries in the United States and the United Kingdom that specialize in bulbs or offer hard-to-find bulbs. Catalogs or lists are available from most. No endorsement is intended, nor is criticism implied of sources not mentioned.

Avon Bulbs
Burnt House Farm
Mid Lambrook
South Petherton
Somerset TA13 5HE
United Kingdom
+44 (0) 1460-242177
http://avonbulbs.com

Brent and Becky's Bulbs
7900 Daffodil Lane
Gloucester, Virginia 23061
(804) 693-3966
http://www.brentandbeckysbulbs.com

Broadleigh Gardens
Bishops Hull
Taunton
Somerset TA4 1AE
United Kingdom
+44 (0) 1823-286231

The Bulb Shop
Fengate Road
West Pinchbeck
Spalding
Lincolnshire PE11 3NE
United Kingdom
+44 (0) 1775-640381
http://thebulbshop.co.uk

Cambridge Bulbs
40 Whittlesford Road
Newton, Cambridge
United Kingdom CB2 5PH
+44 (0) 1223 871760

De Vroomen Holland Garden Products
P.O. Box 189
Russell, Illinois 60075
(847) 395-9911
http:///www.devroomen.com

Dutch Gardens
144 Intervale Road
Burlington, Vermont 05401
(800) 944-2250
http://www.dutchgardens.com

Elkhorn Gardens
8043 San Miguel Canyon Road
Prunedale, CA 93907
(831) 663-1126
http://www.elkhorngardens.com

Heritage Bulb Club
Tullynally Castel
Castlepollard
County Westmeath
Ireland
+353 044 62744
http://www.heritagebulbs.com

John Scheepers
P.O. Box 638
23 Tulip Drive
Bantam, Connecticut 06750
(860) 567-0838
http://www.johnscheepers.com

Klehm's Song Sparrow Perennial Farm
13101 East Rye Road
Avalon, Wisconsin 53505
(800) 533-3715
http://www.songsparrow.com

The Lily Garden
4902 NE 147th Avenue
Vancouver, Washington 98682
(360) 253-6273
http://www.thelilygarden.com

MAS Seed Specialists
4 Pinhills
Wenhill Heights
Calne
Wiltshire SN11 OSA
United Kingdom
+44 (0) 01249-819013
http://www.meadowmania.co.uk

McClure & Zimmerman
Quality Flowerbulb Brokers
P.O. Box 368
108 W. Winnebago Street
Friesland, Wisconsin 53935
(800) 883-6998
http://www.mzbulba

Naturescape British Wild Flowers
Maple Farm
Coach Gap Lane
Langar
Nottinghamshire NG13 9HP
United Kingdom
+44 (0) 1949-860592
http://www.naturescape.co.uk

Old House Gardens
536 Third Street
Ann Arbor, Michigan 48103
(734) 995-1486
http://www.oldhousegardens.com

Orchard Nurseries
Orchard Place, Flint House Road
Three Holes, Wisbech
Cambridgeshire PE14 9JN
United Kingdom
+44 (0) 01354-638613
http://www.orchard-nurseries.co.uk

Plant Delights Nursery
9241 Sauls Road
Raleigh, North Carolina 27603
(919) 772-4794
http://www.plantdelights.com

Pottertons Nursery
Moortown Road
Nettleton, Caistor
Lincolnshire LN7 6HX
United Kingdom
+44 (0) 1472-851714
http://www.pottertons.co.uk

Telos Rare Bulbs
P.O. Box 4147
Arcata, California 95518
www.telosrarebulbs.com

Tile Barn Nursery
Standen Street
Iden Green
Benenden
Kent TN17 4LB
United Kingdom
+44 (0) 1580-240221
http://www.tilebarn-cyclamen.co.uk

Van Zyverden Gardens
12035 Higgins Airport Way
Burlington, Washington 98233
(360) 757-0444
http://www.vanzyverdenusa.com

White Flower Farm
P.O. Box 50
Route 63
Litchfield, Connecticut 06759
(800)503-9624
http://www.whiteflowerfarm.com

Yucca Do Nursery
P.O. Box 907
FM 359 & FM 3346
Hempstead, Texas 77445
(979) 826-4580
http://www.yuccado.com

GLOSSARY

acid having a pH of less than 7.

alkaline having a pH of 7 or above.

alternate arranged on a stem at different heights; not opposite.

anther the pollen-bearing portion of a stamen.

axil the upper angle formed where a leaf is attached to a stem.

basal growing from the base.

basal plate the bottom of the bulb, from which roots emerge.

blade the thin, expanded part of a leaf or petal.

bract a modified, protective leaf usually subtending the flowers.

bulbil a small bulb produced above ground on the stem or inflorescence.

bulblet a small bulb produced below ground on the base of the stem.

capsule a dry pod that holds the seed.

corolla the inner whorl of a flower consisting of petals.

corona a "crown" or cuplike appendage between the corolla and the stamens, as in *Narcissus* (daffodils).

corymb a flat-topped inflorescence in which the outer flowers open first.

crest a ridge, as on the falls of an iris.

cultivar a plant maintained and propagated in cultivation.

deciduous shedding foliage at the end of the growth period; not evergreen.

double having twice the usual number of petals.

fall an outer perianth segment which seems to droop. On an iris, the three outer segments.

filament the stalk of a stamen.

forcing bulbs bringing bulbs into flower ahead of their normal flowering time.

glaucous covered with a white, blue-green, or gray bloom.

herbaceous not woody; dying back to the ground each year.

inflorescence the main flower stem and its flowers.

linear slender, narrow, with more or less parallel edges.

midrib the main rib of a leaf.

naturalized plants which have established colonies and multiply.

neck the upper part of a true bulb from which emerge the stem and leaves.

nectary a gland that secretes nectar.

node the point on a stem where a leaf is attached.

opposite arranged on opposite sides of a stem; not alternate.

outward-facing held horizontally, not upright- or downward-facing.

ovary the female part of the flower containing ovules.

pedicel the stalk of an individual flower.

perianth the outer, usually showy part of a flower, consisting of the corolla and calyx.

petal a modified leaf of the corolla, generally brightly colored.

pistil one of the female reproductive organs, comprising the ovary, style, and stigma.

raceme an inflorescence in which the flowers are borne on individual stalks which are attached to the main stem.

ray florets one of the outer flowers in the head of some plants.

reflexed abruptly curled back, at more than a 90-degree angle.

rootstock an underground fibrous, rhizomatous, or tuberous stem; the roots.

rosette a circular cluster of leaves, often close to or touching the ground.

sepal a segment in the outer whorl of a flower; collectively sepals form the calyx.

spadix a spike of flowers on a thick, often fleshy axis, as in *Arum*.

spathe a conspicuous leaf or bract that subtends a spadix.

spike an inflorescence with flowers that lack stalks.

spur a growth on the perianth.

stamen the male or pollen-producing part of a plant, comprised of the filament and anther.

stigma the tip of the style which receives the pollen.

stolon an underground stem which roots to form new plants.

style the narrow part of the pistil, between the ovary and the stigma.

tepal a perianth segment that cannot be distinguished as either sepal or petal.

terminal at the tip of a stem.

tunic the covering of a bulb or corm, as seen in daffodil bulbs.

umbel an inflorescence with individual flowers arising from a central point, like the spokes of an umbrella.

upward-facing erect; upright.

whorl the placement of leaves in a circle around a plant stem, as in certain lily species.

FURTHER READING

Bales, Suzanne F. 1992. *Bulbs*. Prentice Hall.

Bryan, John, ed. 1995. *Manual of Bulbs*. Timber Press.

Bryan, John. 2002. *Bulbs*. Rev. ed. Timber Press.

Doutt, Richard L. 1994. *Cape Bulbs*. Timber Press.

Elliott, Jack. 1995. *Bulbs for the Rock Garden*. Timber Press.

Ellis, Quin. 1994. *A Bulb for all Seasons*. William Morrow.

Glattstein, Judy. 1994. *The American Gardener's World of Bulbs*. Little, Brown and Company.

Grey-Wilson, Christopher, Brian Mathew, and Marjorie Blamey. 1981. *Bulbs: The Bulbous Plants of Europe and Their Allies*. Collins.

Hill, Lewis, and Nancy Hill. 1994. *Bulbs*. Storey Communications.

Hobbs, Jack, and Terry Hatch. 1994. *The Best Bulbs for Temperate Climates*. Timber Press.

Jeppe, Barbara, and Graham Duncan. 1989. *Spring and Winter Flowering Bulbs of the Cape*. Oxford University Press.

Leeds, Rod. 2000. *The Plantfinder's Guide to Early Bulbs*. Timber Press.

Mathew, Brian. 1997. *Growing Bulbs: The Complete Practical Guide*. Timber Press.

Mathew, Brian. 1973. *Dwarf Bulbs*. Batsford.

Mathew, Brian, and Philip Swindells. 1994. *The Complete Book of Bulbs, Corms, Tubers, and Rhizomes: A Step-By-Step Guide to Nature's Easiest and Most Rewarding Plants*. Reader's Digest Corporation.

McGary, Jane, ed. 2001. *Bulbs of North America*. Timber Press.

Ogden, Scott. 1994. *Garden Bulbs for the South*. Taylor Publishing Company.

Redgrove, Hugh, ed. 1991. *Bulbs and Perennials*. Godwit Press.

Wilder, Louise Beebe. 1990. *Adventures with Hardy Bulbs*. Collier Books, Macmillian.

INDEX

Bold-faced numbers indicate photo pages.